FACTS AMERICA

OUR
SOLAR
SYSTEM

BRIAN JONES AND ANDREW GUTELLE

SMITHMARK

About the authors

Brian Jones is a free-lance author and broadcaster who specializes in astronomy and space exploration. He has published six books on astronomy and has contributed articles to many other books, magazines, and newspapers. Mr. Jones also teaches astronomy at several schools near his home in Bradford, West Yorkshire, United Kingdom.

Andrew Gutelle is a children's author with a strong interest in science and nature. He is a writer for the Emmy Award-winning television series "Reading Rainbow." Mr. Gutelle also created 3-2-1 Contact magazine, winner of a National Magazine Award for Excellence. He is a member of the Writers' Guild of America and the Society of Children's Book Writers.

Editor:
Philip de Ste. Croix

Designer:
Stonecastle Graphics Ltd

Picture research:
Leora Kahn

Coordinating editors:
Andrew Preston
Kristen Schilo

Production:
Ruth Arthur
Sally Connolly
Neil Randles
Andrew Whitelaw

Production editor:
Didi Charney

Director of production:
Gerald Hughes

Typesetter:
Pagesetters Incorporated

Color and monochrome reproduction:
Advance Laser Graphic Arts, Hong Kong

Printed and bound in Hong Kong by
Leefung-Asco Printers Ltd

Text copyright © 1992 SMITHMARK Publishers Inc./
Brian Jones

1992 Colour Library Books Ltd
Godalming Business Centre
Woolsack Way, Godalming
Surrey GU7 1XW, United Kingdom
CLB 2609

This edition published in 1992 by
SMITHMARK Publishers Inc.
112 Madison Avenue
New York, NY 10016 USA

SMITHMARK books are available for bulk purchase for sales promotion and premium use. For details, write or call the manager of special sales, SMITHMARK Publishers Inc., 112 Madison Avenue, New York, NY 10016; (212) 532-6600.

Library of Congress Cataloging-in-Publication Data

Jones, Brian, 1953–
    Facts America. Our solar system / Brian Jones & Andrew Gutelle.
      p. cm.
    Includes bibliographical references and index.
    Summary: Discusses the planets, asteroids, comets, and meteors that make up the solar system.
    ISBN 0-8317-2316-5 (hardcover)
    1. Solar system—Juvenile literature. 2. Astronomy—Juvenile literature. [1. Solar system. 2. Astronomy.] I. Gutelle, Andrew.
II. Title. III. Title: Our solar system.
QB501.3.J64 1992
523.2—dc20   92-9406

This is a picture of the payload bay of the space shuttle Challenger, *taken as it orbited Earth at an altitude of about 17? miles in August 1985. The maj? piece of equipment visible is a telescope that was used to stud? the Sun.*

Contents

1 Our Solar System

On a clear night, hundreds, or even thousands, of stars may be seen in the sky. They appear as tiny points of twinkling light. During the day, they seem to disappear in the bright light of a single star—our Sun.

The Sun is at the center of our Solar System. Moving around it are planets with their moons, plus other objects such as comets and asteroids.

Because the Sun is so much nearer Earth, it seems enormous compared to other stars. Actually, it is an average star in size and age. The Sun has burned brightly since it formed nearly 5 billion years ago.

A STAR IS BORN: Billions of years ago, before the Sun or Earth existed, there was a giant cloud of gas and dust floating in space. Over time, this cloud started to spin and the force of gravity made it begin to break up. The shrinking cloud flattened out. Material within it became more tightly packed together.

As gas and dust collected in the middle of the cloud, the center became hotter and hotter. When the heat and pressure were great enough, they triggered nuclear reactions. A young star glowed with heat and began sending energy into space. The Sun had formed.

Most of the material in that giant solar cloud was used to form the Sun, but outside of it some dust remained. As this material moved around the developing Sun, bits of it collided and started clumping together. The larger clumps began attracting the smaller clumps around them. These collecting masses formed the planets. Other bodies such as comets and asteroids also came together as part of this process. Scientists estimate that it took our Solar System 100 million years to form.

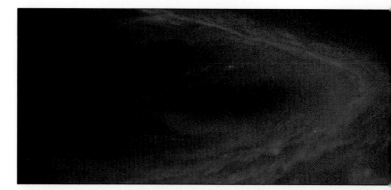

▼ *This diagram shows the nine planets and their distances from the Sun. The four inner planets— Mercury (1), Venus (2), Earth (3), and Mars (4)— are grouped near the Sun. The four gas giants— Jupiter (5), Saturn (6), Uranus (7), and Neptune (8) —and tiny Pluto (9) are much farther away.*

▲ *These drawings show the main stages in the development of our Solar System. The top picture shows a giant cloud of dust and gas. In the middle drawing, the cloud has squeezed together to form a dense center. The planets have begun to cluster around the center. In the bottom picture, the formation of the Sun and planets is complete.*

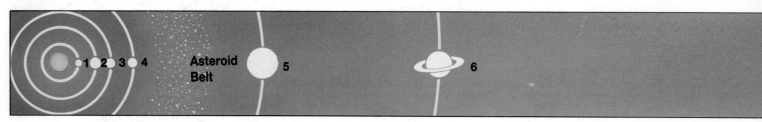

1 2 3 4   Asteroid Belt   5   6

FUTURE STAR SYSTEMS: New stars and solar systems are developing all the time. Scientists have detected giant clouds, called nebulas, which are much like the one that formed our Sun. In recent years, scientists have launched satellites that study regions of star formation deep in space.

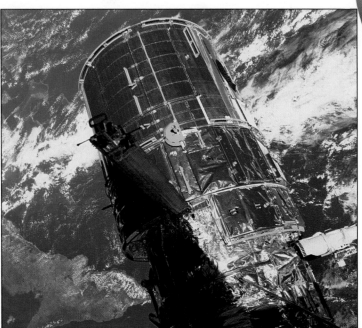

◀ *The Hubble Space Telescope orbits Earth. Satellites often provide the clearest pictures of what lies beyond our planet.*

▼ *This image shows the night sky. The band of stars across the middle is the Milky Way galaxy. Our Solar System is inside this galaxy near its edge.*

▲ *This diagram compares the size of the nine planets in our Solar System. Mercury (1), Venus (2), Earth (3), Mars (4), and Pluto (9) are fairly small. Jupiter (5), Saturn (6), Uranus (7), and Neptune (8) are much larger.*

▲ *This image shows new star systems forming in space. Pictures like this have helped scientists understand how our Solar System began.*

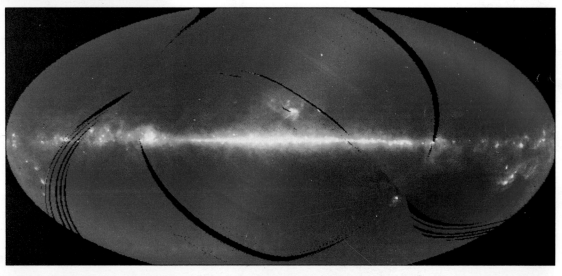

2 Inside the Sun

Although the Sun is an average-size star, it is by far the largest object in our Solar System. It is so big that more than one million Earths could fit inside it easily.

Nearly 98 percent of all the solid material in our Solar System has been collected inside the Sun. Because it is so huge, the Sun's gravity exerts a powerful hold on everything near it. It keeps planets and other objects moving around it in regular orbits.

The Sun is a giant ball of burning gas. It is made up mostly of hydrogen gas, which it slowly is turning into helium gas. This process produces the heat we feel 93 million miles away.

THE SOLAR FURNACE: The Sun is made up of several layers. Its center, or core, is by far its hottest part. Scientists estimate the temperature of the core to be about 27 million degrees Fahrenheit (F). The core is a colossal nuclear furnace. The enormous heat and pressure there turn hydrogen atoms into helium atoms. This process is called fusion. A fusion reaction produces incredible amounts of energy.

The energy in the Sun's core moves out through other layers on its way to the surface. It passes through the radiation zone and then the convection zone. Finally, it reaches the Sun's surface, or photosphere. Although much cooler than its core, temperatures here average 10,000° F.

The Sun's energy is created ▶ *in its center, or core. The energy rises to the surface, where it escapes into space as light and heat.*

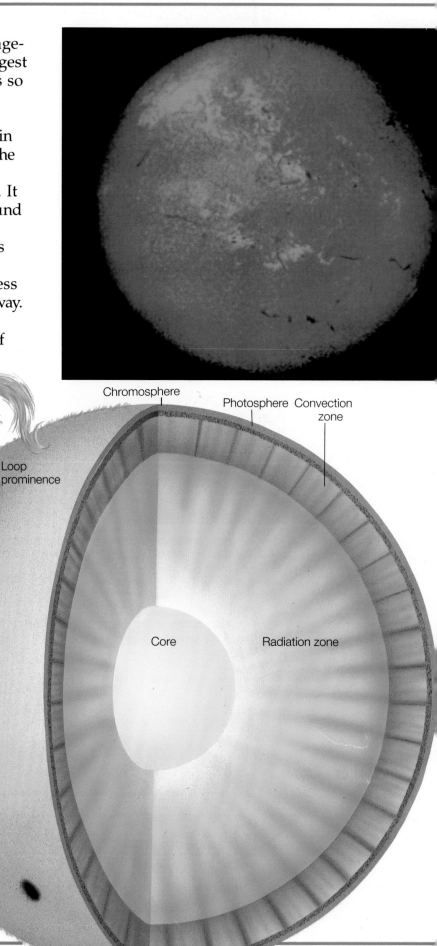

Chromosphere

Photosphere Convection zone

Loop prominence

Sunspots

Core

Radiation zone

Eruptive prominence

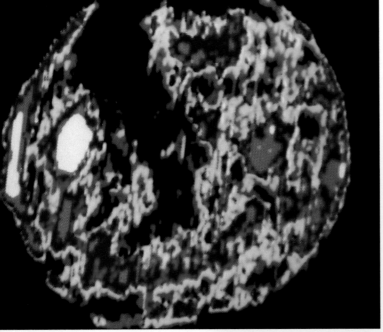

Most of the Sun's energy is released into space as light and heat. As this energy leaves the surface, it must pass through the regions of the Sun's atmosphere, including the chromosphere and the corona.

THE END OF THE SUN: Like any furnace, the Sun uses up material as it burns. The Sun burns up millions of tons of matter every second! Someday, the Sun will use up all its matter, but that time is far in the future. Scientists estimate that the Sun has been burning for 4.5 billion years. They expect that it will continue to burn as it has for another 4.5 billion years.

In its final stages, the Sun will go through a series of changes. The yellow star will first expand to form a red star, called a red giant. This enormous star will reach into space as far as Earth's orbit. As it uses up its remaining fuel, the Sun then will become smaller and smaller. In the end, it will be an incredibly heavy object, no larger than Earth.

◄ *This photograph shows the Sun's chromosphere—the area just above its surface.*

▲ *People have always wondered about the Sun and stars. One early belief held that the stars were fixed to a solid dome in the sky.*

▲ *This image shows temperature differences in the Sun's corona. The dark area, in the shape of a boot, is cooler than the areas around it.*

Like a tongue of fire, a solar ► *prominence erupts out through the Sun's chromosphere. A large prominence may rise half a million miles above the Sun's surface.*

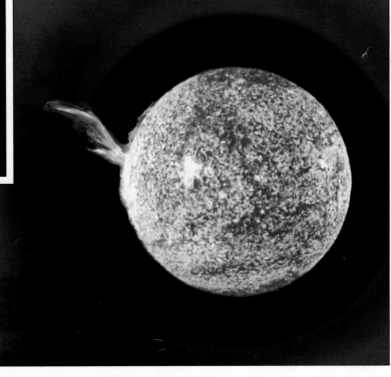

The Active Sun

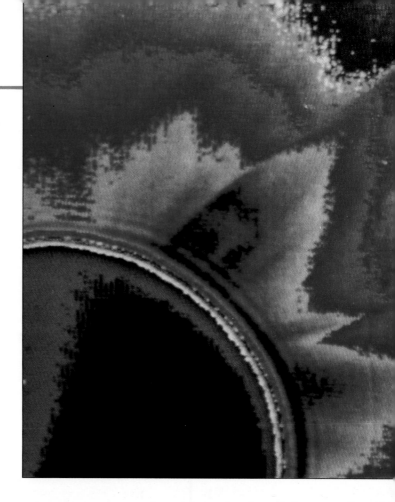

The incredible heat in the Sun's center produces changes on its surface. From the star's core, giant columns of fiery gas shoot to the photosphere. They rise at speeds of more than 1,000 miles per hour. This constant churning of gas gives the Sun a granular appearance.

SPOTS ON THE SURFACE: The best-known features of the solar surface are sunspots. Changes in the Sun's magnetic field cause these stormy regions to develop. Sunspots appear as dark patches on the photosphere. They are thousands of degrees cooler than the areas around them.

Sunspots come in many sizes. A typical one is about the size of Earth. The spots seem to move across the surface of the Sun. Sunspots usually last about two months. They can appear at any time but seem to follow a definite pattern. The Sun breaks out in an unusual number of spots every 11 years.

FLARES AND PROMINENCES: Many spectacular sights often appear near sunspots. At times, huge columns of fiery gas rise above the surface of the Sun. These are called solar prominences. Some prominences hang above the surface for many days. Others send huge columns of gas blasting into space at high speed. An explosive

prominence can shoot hundreds of thousands of miles into space!

Sunspots are also the areas from which solar flares appear. In these thin columns of hot gas, temperatures can soar to several millions of degrees within a very short time. A typical flare lasts about 20 minutes. During that time, it sends out enormous amounts of radiation.

The activity on the Sun's surface can be detected in the atmosphere that surrounds the star. Flares light up the chromosphere, which lies just above the Sun's surface. Prominences rise even higher through the corona, which lies above the chromosphere.

NEVER STARE AT THE SUN: Because the Sun is so active, *it is important that you never look directly at it!* Certain kinds of radiation that it produces will damage the human eye. Injury can happen after staring at the Sun for even a short period of time.

◄ *The Sun's upper atmosphere is called the corona. In this picture of an eclipse, the corona appears as a pinkish haze.*

This image reveals activity ► *above the Sun's surface. At times, hot gases form arching loops.*

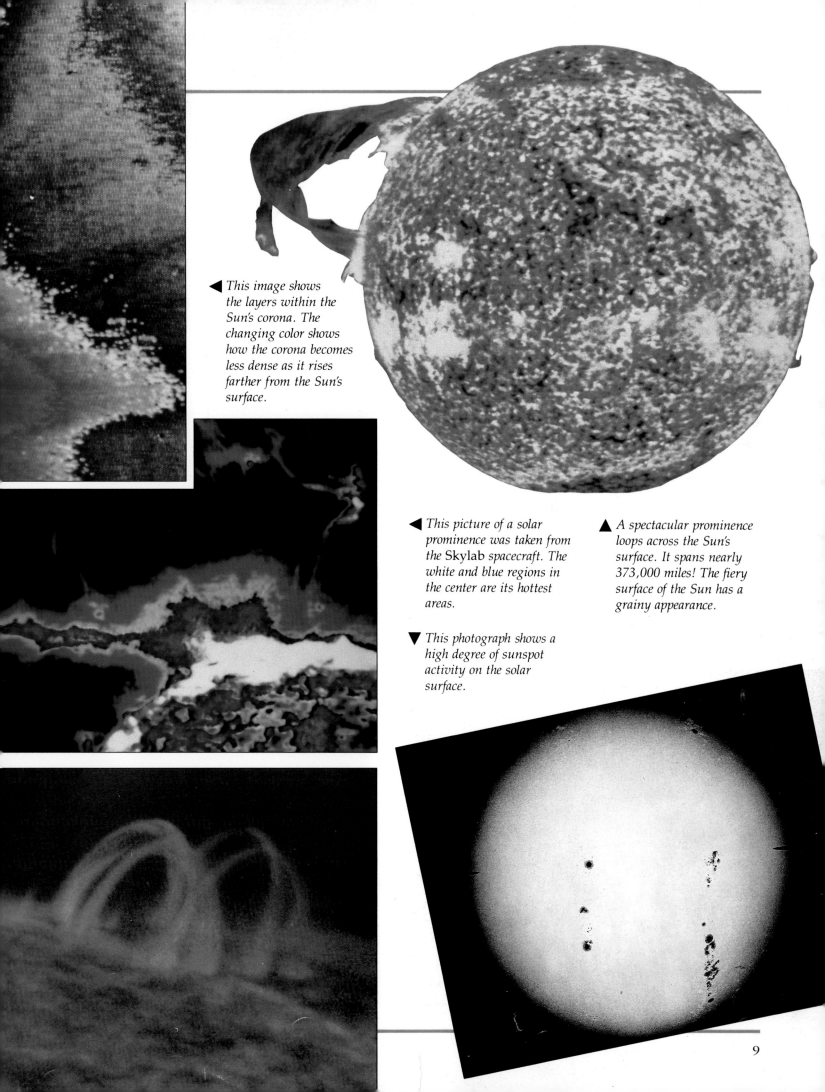

◀ This image shows the layers within the Sun's corona. The changing color shows how the corona becomes less dense as it rises farther from the Sun's surface.

◀ This picture of a solar prominence was taken from the Skylab spacecraft. The white and blue regions in the center are its hottest areas.

▲ A spectacular prominence loops across the Sun's surface. It spans nearly 373,000 miles! The fiery surface of the Sun has a grainy appearance.

▼ This photograph shows a high degree of sunspot activity on the solar surface.

Auroras

Earth orbits the Sun from an average distance of 93 million miles. Although this sounds very far, it is not, given that our Solar System is billions of miles wide.

From its position in space, Earth receives from the Sun the light and heat necessary for plant and animal life. The explosive, active Sun also sends out other forms of energy that continually reach and influence our planet.

GLOWING NIGHT LIGHTS: Among the more spectacular results of the Sun's activities are auroras. At times, these shimmering curtains of colored light fill the night sky. Auroras appear in many colors including red, green, violet, and blue. They may cause the sky to glow faintly, or they may appear in dazzling, ribbonlike patterns.

Auroras are seen nearer the poles of Earth. The aurora borealis, or northern lights, is the name given to an aurora found in the north. The aurora australis, or southern lights, glows in the southern sky.

SOLAR WIND AND A MAGNETIC EARTH: The turbulent Sun is constantly sending radiation into space. This solar wind of charged particles, called ions, streams toward Earth. During periods of increased sunspot activity, solar flares send out more radiation than usual.

Movements within Earth cause our world to act like a giant magnet. Around the planet, a magnetic field influences any charged particles that come near Earth. Scientists call this magnetic field the magnetosphere.

As the solar wind nears Earth, the upper region of the magnetosphere deflects most ions. However, some particles are pulled down through these upper layers. They settle in the sky in two regions called the Van Allen radiation belts.

Usually, the particles of solar wind remain within the Van Allen belts. However, increased sunspot activity can overload the belts with radiation. When that happens, ions are released into the atmosphere. As these high-energy particles collide with gas in the atmosphere, they produce auroras.

People living in Canada or the northern United States often can see auroras. On a clear, dark night, look for a glow in the northern sky. The best time of year to see auroras is during the winter.

This blue-green aurora ▶
was photographed from a
spacecraft. Bits of red can be
seen in its upper regions.
Auroras at higher altitudes
tend to be redder in color.

▼ Many auroras appear as
glowing light along the
horizon. An orbiting space
shuttle photographed this
wide aurora.

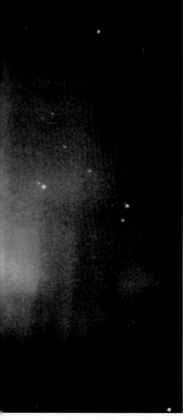

▲ The most spectacular
auroras appear as
shimmering curtains of
colored light.

◀ A blue-white aurora lights
up the sky in Finland.

This diagram shows how an ▶
aurora occurs. Most particles
of solar wind are deflected and
swept away by Earth's
magnetosphere, which stretches
into space. Some charged
particles reach the Van Allen
radiation belts. When too
many particles fill this region,
they release into Earth's
atmosphere and cause an
aurora.

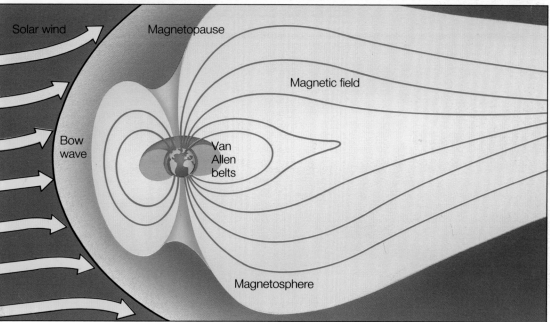

Solar wind

Magnetopause

Magnetic field

Bow
wave

Van
Allen
belts

Magnetosphere

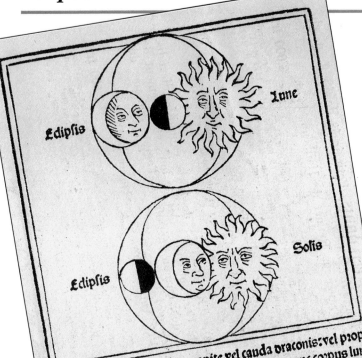

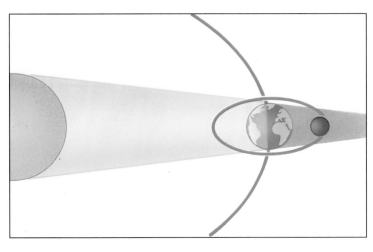

▲ This diagram illustrates a lunar eclipse. As Earth passes between the Sun and the Moon, its shadow falls on the lunar surface.

▼ Eclipses have always aroused great interest among professional and amateur astronomers.

▲ Eclipses have fascinated people for centuries. This diagram made in 1642 shows both a solar and a lunar eclipse.

▼ In this photograph, the Moon is in a partial eclipse. Sunlight passing through Earth's atmosphere gives the Moon a faint reddish color.

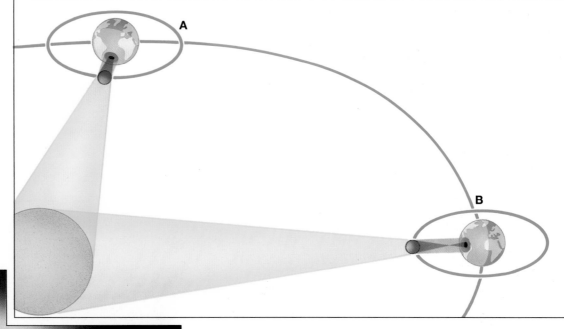

The Sun is enormous when compared to the Moon. Yet these two bodies often seem about the same size when viewed in the sky above Earth. This illusion is the result of the Moon's being much closer to Earth.

As Earth and the Moon move around the Sun, they constantly change position. At certain times, the Moon or Earth blocks out the light of the Sun. When that happens, we see an eclipse.

SOLAR ECLIPSE: During a solar eclipse, the Moon passes between Earth and the Sun. As it does, the Moon prevents sunlight from reaching Earth. If the eclipse is total, the entire Sun seems to disappear. Sometimes the Moon is in a position to block only a portion of the Sun.

When that happens, we see a partial eclipse.

As many as five partial eclipses of the Sun are seen somewhere on Earth every year. A total solar eclipse is less common. One occurs every year or two. It can last as long as seven and a half minutes, although most last two or three minutes. Since eclipses can only be seen from a small area of Earth's surface, people travel great distances to witness these rare events.

LUNAR ECLIPSE: During a lunar eclipse, Earth passes between the Sun and the Moon. It is the shadow of Earth falling on the Moon that causes the Moon to darken. Lunar eclipses are also partial or total depending on the position of Earth.

A typical lunar eclipse lasts much longer than a solar eclipse does. It may take six hours for the Moon to pass completely through Earth's shadow. The eclipse can be total for more than an hour and a half of that time. Lunar eclipses are visible from much more of Earth's surface than are solar eclipses.

During a total lunar eclipse, the Moon darkens but remains visible in the night sky. Although Earth is blocking the Sun, some of the Sun's light reaches the Moon through Earth's atmosphere. The eclipsed Moon continues to shine with a reddish brown color.

3 Earth and the Moon

Earth and its Moon are an unusual pair in our Solar System. Most planets with moons have more than one natural satellite orbiting them. Planets are also usually much larger than their moons.

The Moon is Earth's only satellite, and the two are surprisingly similar in size. Earth's diameter is not quite four times larger than its Moon's. The Earth's mass is about eighty-one times that of its Moon. Most planets in our Solar System are hundreds or thousands of times more massive than their moons are.

In part because of its relatively large size, the Moon's influence can be felt on Earth. The gravitational pull of the Moon causes the tides in our oceans. Although the Moon produces no light of its own, it shines with reflected light from the Sun and helps people and animals find their way at night.

A POWERFUL ATTRACTION: The Moon takes just over 27 days to complete one orbit of Earth. Our planet exerts a strong gravitational hold on the Moon. As a result, the same side of the Moon faces Earth throughout its orbit. Nearly half of the Moon is always hidden from view.

It is only in recent years that the mysterious far side of the Moon has been seen. Spacecraft have sent back pictures showing craters, mountains, and lunar seas on the dark side. Unmanned space probes and those with astronauts on board have reached the Moon and made other discoveries. They have changed our knowledge of Earth and its Moon.

▲ *Although the Moon is clearly visible from Earth, the best view is from approaching spacecraft. This Apollo 13 photograph reveals several dark patches, called lunar maria, or seas.*

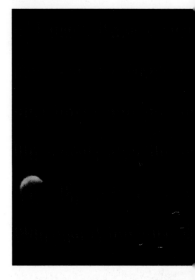

The Moon often appears ▶ *as a crescent in the night sky. In this photograph from Voyager 1, Earth and the Moon appear as twin crescents.*

HOW THE MOON DEVELOPED: For hundreds of years, ideas have been put forward to explain how the Moon formed. One popular theory suggested that the Moon was once part of the young Earth. While Earth was forming, a piece broke off and went into orbit. Another idea suggested that the Moon developed in another part of our Solar System. When its orbit brought it close to Earth, the planet's gravity captured it.

Lunar rocks and soil samples have proven both theories wrong. The current theory suggests the Moon formed around the same time as Earth. During this period, the young, rapidly spinning Earth collided with another object. The core of the body that hit Earth became part of our planet. The lighter material shot into space. It began orbiting Earth and eventually collected to form the Moon.

Missions to the Moon ▼ *reveal much about Earth as well. Apollo 17 astronauts took this photograph during their lunar mission.*

▲ *The Soviet space station Salyut 7 drifts in orbit above Earth. Spacecraft in orbit provide vital information about the Earth-Moon system.*

▼ *An Apollo 11 photograph shows Earth rising over a lunar sea. Earth shines with reflected sunlight.*

Moon Panorama

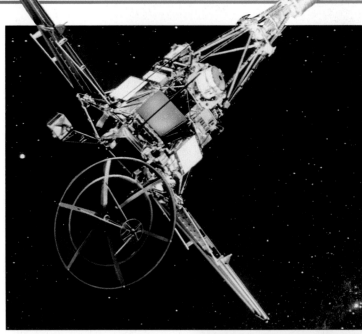

The Moon's surface can be studied easily with the naked eye. Long ago, astronomers on Earth stared at the Moon and tried to explain the details they could see.

SEAS WITHOUT WATER: The Moon's surface includes several dark patches. The first astronomers thought these were huge expanses of water. They gave them names such as the Sea of Tranquillity, the Bay of Rainbows, and the Lake of Death. However, we now know there is no water on the moon. These lunar seas are actually smooth, flat plains.

The lunar plains formed 3.5 billion years ago, when lava poured out from the interior of the Moon. The lava flowed into the lowlands, covering about 15 percent of the lunar surface.

CRATER-SCARRED SURFACES: The dark plains are quite different from the brighter areas, which cover the rest of the Moon. While the plains are fairly smooth, thousands of craters cover the highlands. Some craters have mountainous edges or peaks rising from their centers. The largest ones can be seen from Earth without the aid of a telescope.

Most of the craters formed during a period when meteors rained down on the Moon. Since there are few craters in the lowlands, these meteor showers must have occurred before lava flowed from the Moon's interior.

Unlike Earth, the Moon has no atmosphere. Its surface is not constantly worn away by wind or rain erosion. Except for rare impacts of meteorites in more recent times, the Moon has not changed at all.

Samples of Moon rock tell a story of a world that formed long ago. When scientists study these rocks, it is as if they were looking back billions of years to the early ages of our Solar System.

▲ Ranger *probes surveyed the Moon prior to the manned landings. The Ranger craft sent back pictures of the lunar surface before crash landing.*

Unlike the Rangers, ▶ Surveyor *probes landed softly on the Moon. They provided pictures of potential landing areas and analyzed lunar soil.*

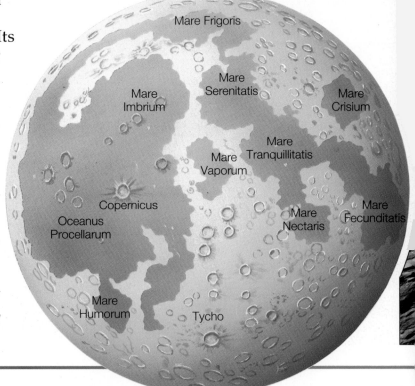

The features on this lunar ▶ *drawing can be seen from Earth with the naked eye. Most names appear in Latin. Craters like Tycho and Copernicus have been named for famous astronomers.*

Mare Frigoris

Mare Imbrium

Mare Serenitatis

Mare Crisium

Mare Vaporum

Mare Tranquillitatis

Copernicus

Mare Nectaris

Mare Fecunditatis

Oceanus Procellarum

Mare Humorum

Tycho

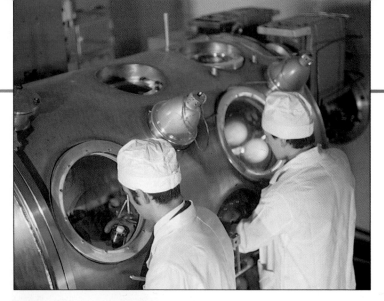

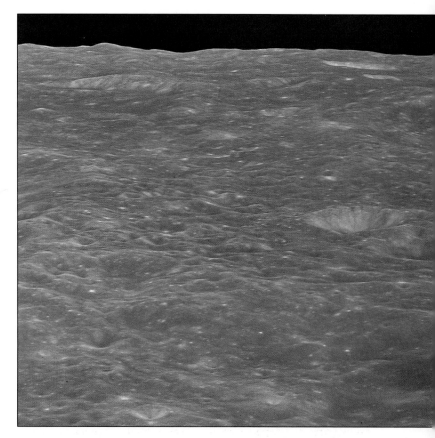

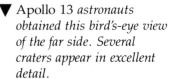 The unmanned Luna 20 landed on the Moon and then returned a capsule to Earth. Here, scientists examine rock samples brought back by the spacecraft.

Apollo 8 astronauts ▶ photographed the far side of the Moon. Pictures like this have helped scientists map the Moon's once-hidden half.

▼ Apollo 13 astronauts obtained this bird's-eye view of the far side. Several craters appear in excellent detail.

▼ The large crater in the foreground is named Goclenius. It measures about 44 miles in diameter.

Ever since people began discovering other worlds in space, they have dreamed of journeying to them. So far, the Moon is the only place in our Solar System where we have realized that dream.

In 1961, President John F. Kennedy set a target for America's space program. The United States would strive to land an astronaut on the Moon by the end of the decade. Project Gemini, a series of space missions close to Earth, would lay the groundwork. Then, following Gemini's success, the Apollo space program would progress all the way to the Moon.

A HISTORIC LAUNCH: On July 16, 1969, *Apollo 11* lifted off from the Kennedy Space Center. Four days later, *Apollo's* lunar module (LM) touched down in the Sea of Tranquillity. That triumphant landing established a new frontier in the exploration of space.

Five more successful landings followed the *Apollo 11* mission. They were the result of years of effort poured into the American space program. The Apollo program cost more than $20 billion and employed the services of half a million people.

BEFORE APOLLO: The *Ranger, Orbiter,* and *Surveyor* probes were the first U.S. spacecraft sent to the Moon. These unmanned flights helped the National Aeronautics and Space Administration (NASA) select possible landing sites for the manned flights. These missions also gave NASA scientists a taste of what lunar conditions would be like.

The first astronauts to orbit the Moon flew on *Apollo 8.* After that success, *Apollo 9* astronauts launched into Earth orbit a command and service module (CSM) and a lunar module. These vehicles and other equipment would be used during future lunar landings. Astronauts put the equipment through a series of careful tests.

The *Apollo 10* flight was the final rehearsal. While orbiting the Moon, astronauts separated the lunar module from the command and service module. They flew low over the Sea of Tranquillity. When they redocked successfully, the stage was set for the most famous lunar flight of all.

▲ Apollo 11 *Astronaut Edwin "Buzz" Aldrin is pictured here inside the lunar module during the first manned lunar landing mission.*

▼ *The lunar module rises above the Sea of Tranquillity. Earth shines above the Moon's horizon.*

▲ Buzz Aldrin leaves an American flag and dozens of footprints on the lunar surface.

▲ An Apollo 11 astronaut sets up an experiment. Apollo astronauts left many experiments on the lunar surface.

▼ In this famous photograph of Buzz Aldrin, astronaut Neil Armstrong is reflected in Aldrin's visor.

▲ The command and service module orbits the Moon during the Apollo 15 space flight.

First Moon Landing

The astronauts on the historic flight of *Apollo 11* were Michael Collins, Neil Armstrong, and Buzz Aldrin. Collins remained in orbit on the CSM. On July 21, 1969, Armstrong and Aldrin boarded the lunar module, which had been named the *Eagle*. They flew to the landing site and gently touched down in the Sea of Tranquillity. At that moment, people on Earth heard Aldrin report the news: "Tranquillity Base here," he said. "The *Eagle* has landed."

THE FIRST STEPS: Four hours after they landed, the astronauts put on their spacesuits and life-support systems. Neil Armstrong carefully guided himself out through the narrow hatchway and down a ladder to the lunar surface. He placed his foot on the surface. "That's one small step for a man, one giant leap for mankind," he said.

Aldrin followed Armstrong. Between them, they spent almost four hours on the lunar surface. They planted a flag and secured a plaque to commemorate the occasion. Then they set up several experiments on the Moon and collected nearly 50 pounds of lunar soil and rock samples.

When they had finished their work, the two

◀ *Rising on a pillar of flame, the* Saturn V *rocket carries* Apollo 13 *into space. This mission aborted prior to its Moon landing.*

▲ Apollo 15 *astronaut James Irwin boards the lunar rover. Irwin and David Scott explored nearly 17 miles of the lunar surface.*

astronauts boarded the *Eagle* and blasted off the Moon. They successfully docked with Collins in the CSM. Following a crucial engine burn that took them out of lunar orbit, they headed for home. The astronauts splashed down in the Pacific Ocean eight days after their mission had begun.

MORE APOLLO FLIGHTS FOLLOW: Later Apollo missions built on the success of *Apollo 11*. Although the *Apollo 13* flight had to be aborted, five other missions landed on the Moon. On the final three Apollo flights, astronauts used the lunar roving vehicle (LRV). This ten-foot-long cart allowed astronauts to explore much more of the lunar surface.

Apollo 17 was the last manned flight to the Moon. Although very expensive, the Apollo program did provide immense scientific gains. A dozen astronauts explored over 60 miles of the lunar surface. They collected 850 pounds of rock and soil for analysis and left a large number of experiments on the surface. The Apollo astronauts also took over 30,000 photographs. Most importantly, they fulfilled the dream of manned exploration of our Solar System.

▲ Apollo 17 *Astronaut Schmitt works on the Moon. This 1972 mission was the final flight in the successful Apollo series.*

▼ *John Young poses with the lunar rover, the lunar module, and an American flag. Apollo astronauts snapped thousands of pictures.*

Harrison Schmitt uses a ▶ *scoop to gather rocks. The Apollo 17 mission collected 249 pounds of rock and soil samples.*

Earth: A Shifting Planet

It may seem that the land beneath our feet is fixed and never changing. In truth, Earth's huge landmasses are in constant motion across the surface of our planet. Earth's continents have been drifting apart in this way for millions of years.

A SOFT CORE AND A HARD CRUST: Earth is an active, living planet. Its center is made up of liquid, or molten, rock. The outer crust is made up of a number of giant rafts of rocks. These 25-mile-thick plates float on the planet's liquid center. Some plates carry continents, which move very slowly across the planet's surface. The process that moves them is called plate tectonics.

Along the ocean floor lies a string of volcanoes. They sit along huge ridges, or faults, that wrap around the planet. As Earth ejects molten material from its core, the plates move and drift.

The constant eruption of material from Earth's interior forces the plates to move away from one another. Sometimes, moving plates collide. When this happens, one plate can be forced below the other, producing giant trenches along the ocean floor. One plate can also rub against another; this is what is happening along the San Andreas Fault in California. Regions like this are the scenes of violent movements in Earth's crust, which cause earthquakes.

The rate at which continents are moving apart is no more than a few inches per year. Although this may seem slow, imagine the effect it has had over millions of years.

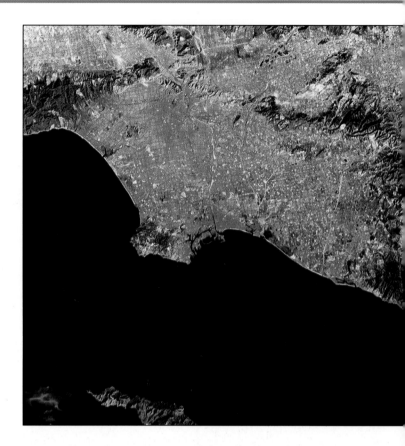

FROM SUPERCONTINENT TO SEVEN: Long ago, all Earth's landmasses formed a single supercontinent, known as Pangaea. Around 200 million years ago, this continent broke up. It is believed that Pangaea split into two sections. While one section drifted north, the other moved south. Over time, the northern section formed Europe, North America, and most of Asia. The southern section divided into the regions that today we know as India, Australia, Antarctica, Africa, and South America.

THE VIEW FROM ABOVE: One of the best ways to study Earth is to view it from space. Satellites such as *Landsat* orbit the planet, collecting data and producing dramatic pictures. They illustrate the natural and human-made changes that constantly alter the surface of our planet.

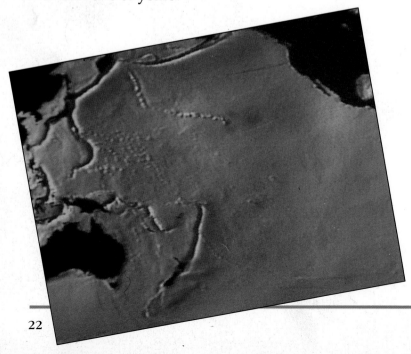

◀ *A* Seasat *satellite created this map of the Pacific Basin. Eruptions along ridges on the ocean floor slowly push continents apart.*

An iceberg breaks away ▶ *from the Ross Ice Shelf in Antarctica. Satellite images record activities in distant regions of Earth.*

◄ *A* Landsat *image shows Los Angeles, California, from a height of 438 miles. In this false-color image, built-up areas appear in shades of blue. The vegetation in parks and agricultural areas is red.*

Landsat *images help detect and monitor pollution on Earth. This picture of a spreading oil slick in the Persian Gulf was taken in 1991 during the Gulf War.* ►

The mountainous regions ► *of Tennessee appear in a crumpled pattern in this* Landsat *image.*

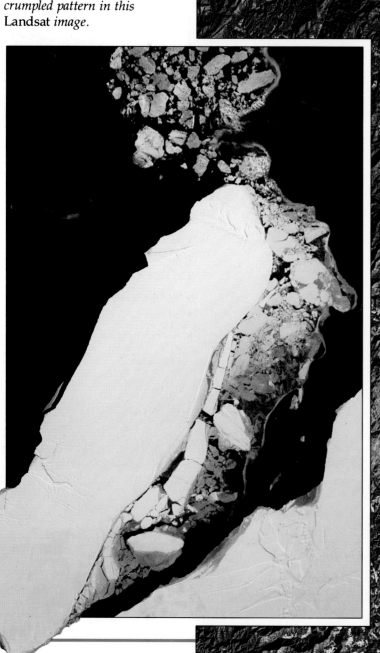

Earth: Air and Water

Earth is a spectacular sight when viewed from space. Because water covers so much of our planet's surface, it appears as a bright blue ball. Landmasses, clearly visible most of the time, disappear below swirling clouds that form in Earth's atmosphere. The water on the planet and the mix of gases in its air make our world uniquely suitable for living things.

WORLD OF WATER: Over 70 percent of Earth's surface is covered with water. In addition to filling the oceans, water is found frozen in the polar ice caps. Water exists on other planets in our Solar System. On Venus, it is locked up in the planet's atmosphere. Mars is also thought to contain water frozen solid beneath the planet's surface. Only on Earth is so much water found in liquid form.

A GLOBAL GREENHOUSE: Earth's atmosphere is made up of a combination of gases. Nitrogen accounts for 77 percent of the air, and oxygen, another 21 percent. The remaining 2 percent is filled by several gases, including carbon dioxide.

Carbon dioxide is a "greenhouse" gas. It traps heat from the Sun and holds it in the atmosphere, much the way glass in a garden greenhouse does. Until recently, the amount of carbon dioxide in our atmosphere had been very small. After warming Earth, the Sun's heat could easily escape back into space.

The amount of carbon dioxide in our atmosphere is slowly increasing. When people burn fuels such as oil and coal, the gas is released into the atmosphere. The gradual increase in carbon dioxide is leading to the so-called greenhouse effect. As carbon dioxide traps heat in the atmosphere, average temperatures around the world slowly rise.

Many scientists are concerned about this global warming. If unchecked, it could produce serious changes on our planet. Rising temperatures could melt portions of the polar ice caps. This change, in turn, would produce a rise in the average sea level across the globe. Many low-lying areas of Earth would be flooded.

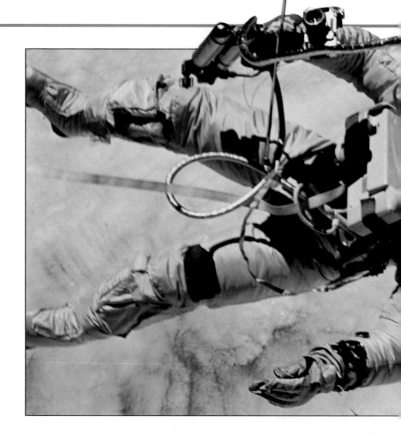

▲ *Astronaut Ed White walks in space above cloud-covered Earth. Water is a critical component of the planet's surface and of its atmosphere.*

▼ *A view of Earth taken by a satellite shows weather patterns that sweep across the oceans and continents.*

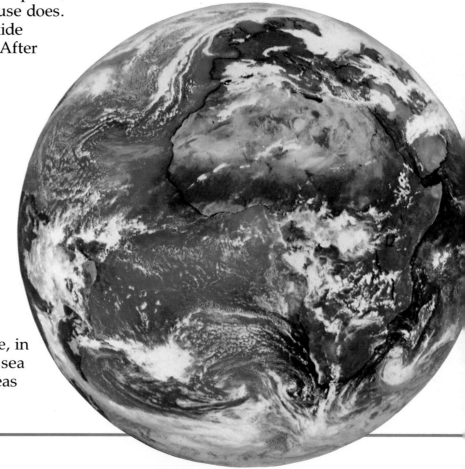

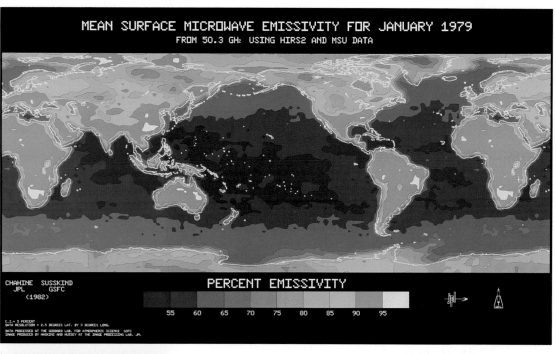

MEAN SURFACE MICROWAVE EMISSIVITY FOR JANUARY 1979
FROM 50.3 GHz USING HIRS2 AND MSU DATA

PERCENT EMISSIVITY

55 60 65 70 75 80 85 90 95

CHAHINE SUSSKIND
JPL GSFC
(1982)

C.I.= 3 PERCENT
DATA RESOLUTION = 2.5 DEGREES LAT. BY 3 DEGREES LONG.
DATA PROCESSED AT THE GODDARD LAB. FOR ATMOSPHERIC SCIENCE GSFC
IMAGE PRODUCED BY HASKINS AND HUSSEY AT THE IMAGE PROCESSING LAB. JPL.

▲ *Maps like this help determine the extent of sea ice and snow cover on our planet. Much of Earth's water is locked in ice and snow.*

▼ *The* Skylab *space station orbits some 250 miles above Earth. Astronauts on space stations spend much longer periods of time studying changes on our home planet.*

▲ *The* Topex/Poseidon *satellite will spend several years mapping ocean currents, wave heights, and seabed shapes.*

◄ *A satellite map shows the hole in the ozone layer above Antarctica. It is the dark area at the center of this picture. The expanding hole in Earth's atmosphere is of concern to people worldwide.*

The Inner Planets

4

The planets in our Solar System are often divided into two groups. Nearer the Sun are four smaller planets—Mercury, Venus, Earth, and Mars. Farther away are the larger gas giants—Jupiter, Saturn, Uranus, and Neptune. Pluto, although much smaller, is grouped with the outer planets.

LIQUID CORES AND ROCKY CRUSTS: Earth and the other inner planets have many traits in common. These small, dense planets are made up of rocky material. Because of their makeup, scientists call the planets terrestrial, which means Earth-like. At the center of each of these planets is a core of molten iron.

The surfaces of the four inner planets were similar when our Solar System formed. Over time, forces at work on these worlds have changed each planet in its own way. The surfaces of all four were bombarded with meteorites long ago and covered with craters. The scars of this time still can be seen on Mercury and Mars. However, weather systems on Earth and Venus have worn away signs of these ancient craters.

Water has played an important part in the shaping of Earth's surface; the same appears true on Mars. Flowing water may have carved the many channels that have been detected in the dry Martian landscape. There is no liquid water on Mars, but there may be water frozen beneath the planet's surface.

When the inner planets first formed, they had atmospheres of helium and hydrogen gas. But then, enormous solar winds blew with hurricane force from the new Sun. They carried the planets' atmospheres into space. After a million years, the winds died down and other changes began to take place. The planets' molten centers gave off gases that eventually formed new atmospheres.

CHANGES IN ATMOSPHERES: Because it is so close to the Sun, Mercury remains an airless planet. The air on Mars is very thin. Both Earth and

▲ Radar-mapping missions have provided detailed information about the surface of Venus. This picture shows the highlands named Aphrodite Terra.

▼ The inner planets have dense cores of iron. This diagram shows how much of each planet is its core. Our Moon also has an iron core.

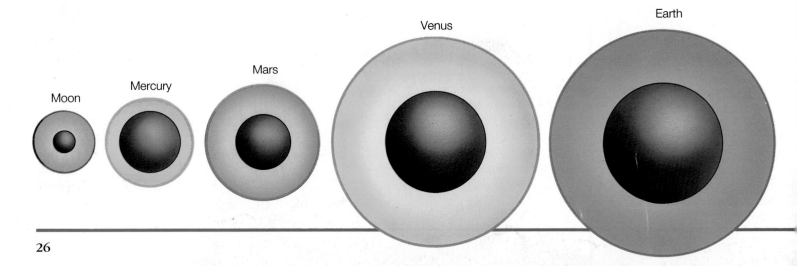

Moon   Mercury   Mars   Venus   Earth

THE TERRESTRIAL PLANETS					
Planet	Diameter miles (km)	Distance From Sun miles (km)	Sidereal Period (year)	Axial Rotation Period	Number of Satellites
Mercury	3,032 (4,880)	36,000,000 (58,000,000)	87.97 days	58.65 days	0
Venus	7,521 (12,104)	67,110,000 (108,000,000)	224.70 days	243.01 days	0
Earth	7,926 (12,756)	92,960,000 (149,600,000)	365.265 days	23.93 hours	1
Mars	4,223 (6,796)	141,600,000 (227,900,000)	686.98 days	24.62 hours	2

Venus have substantial atmospheres. The dense atmosphere on Venus is made up primarily of carbon dioxide. Our view of that planet is blocked by thick clouds, which are probably caused by volcanic eruptions. These clouds are responsible for a runaway greenhouse effect on Venus. Temperatures there are higher than on any other planet or moon in our Solar System.

Mercury's surface is ▶ heavily cratered, like our Moon's.

▲ *This huge canyon on Mars is larger than any on Earth.*

▲ *The unmanned* **Mars Observer** *spacecraft will provide detailed information about the Martian atmosphere. Mars may be the next world visited by humans.*

◀ *Earth is unique because of the free-flowing water on its surface. Water continues to shape and change the planet.*

Mercury

Mercury, the planet nearest the Sun, is small and very hard to see. Most of the time, it is hidden by the Sun's light. At times, it appears as a starry dot of light above the horizon. Even then, people can only see Mercury in the east just before sunrise or in the west after sunset.

A HOT, HEAVY PLANET: Mercury is only slightly larger than our Moon, but it is a densely packed planet. Because its iron core is very large, the tiny planet weighs nearly as much as Earth does. Temperatures on Mercury's surface can reach a sizzling 800° F. With no atmosphere to hold that heat, the temperature at night can plummet to -292° F.

Viewed through a telescope, Mercury remains a mystery. It appears as a tiny, fuzzy ball of light. Details on the surface cannot be seen, and until recently, little was known of the Sun's nearest neighbor.

Italian astronomer Giovanni Schiaparelli made one of the first detailed studies of the planet. During the 1880s, he attempted to chart the planet. These sketchy charts were improved upon by French astronomer Eugenios Antoniadi 40 years later.

Schiaparelli and Antoniadi thought that Mercury spun once on its axis each time it orbited the Sun. This would mean that the planet

◀ Italian astronomer Giovanni Schiaparelli observed Mercury from 1881 to 1889. He drew up the first charts of the planet.

▲ Astronomers study Mercury, Venus, and Jupiter from the roof of Paris Observatory in 1868. Even with a telescope, Mercury is hard to see.

◄ *Mercury is named for the Roman messenger god. The symbol seen above his staff in this 16th-century drawing is also the symbol for the planet.*

▼ *Scientists check* Mariner 10 *prior to launch. This space probe's successful mission answered many questions about the planet.*

This photograph of Mercury is ► *made up of 18 separate pictures taken by* Mariner 10. *The surface resembles the cratered highlands of the Moon.*

always kept the same side turned toward the Sun. We now know this is not the case. Mercury spins on its axis every 58.65 days, so its entire surface receives sunlight at some time or another.

▼ *The crater at the center of this* Mariner 10 *image is about 19 miles wide. The spacecraft took 2,800 pictures of the planet.*

MARINER 10 FLIES BY MERCURY: Many of the mysteries of Mercury were finally solved by *Mariner 10.* This unmanned space probe, launched in 1973, made three passes near the planet during the next two years. *Mariner 10* sent back detailed information about the planet.

Mariner 10 showed that Mercury's surface is covered with thousands of craters. Mountains, ridges, and valleys were also seen. Giant wrinkles in the planet's crust have formed cliffs that wind hundreds of miles over the landscape. Photographs from *Mariner 10* have allowed scientists to chart nearly half the planet's surface.

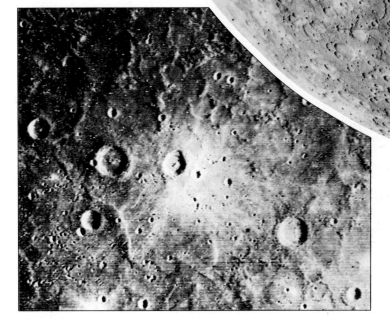

After the Sun and the Moon, Venus is the brightest object in the sky. At the nearest point of its orbit, the planet comes within 25 million miles of Earth. The thick clouds that surround the planet reflect the Sun's light so that Venus appears particularly bright. Since the planet shines before sunrise or just after sunset, people have nicknamed Venus both the Morning Star and the Evening Star.

EARTH'S SISTER PLANET?: Long ago, people thought of Venus and Earth as twins. Venus is the planet nearest ours, and the two worlds are similar in size. People imagined that hidden beneath its thick clouds were lush plants and lots of water.

We know now that these early ideas couldn't have been more wrong. The clouds of Venus are made up of poisonous sulfuric acid. There is no trace of water on the planet's surface. The intense heat and the carbon dioxide that blankets the planet make plant life impossible.

Scientists who study the greenhouse effect on Earth can see its ultimate influence on Venus. That planet's atmosphere is made up almost entirely of carbon dioxide. The gas is packed close to the planet's surface where it traps and holds the Sun's heat. As a result, temperatures on Venus soar to 840° F!

▲ *The Soviet* Venera 4 *probe is seen here in assembly. The* Venera *probes have sent back information about our nearest planetary neighbor.*

▼ *The* Pioneer-Venus *is being prepared for launch The American spacecraft mapped most of Venus and studied the planet's atmosphere.*

SPACECRAFT VISIT VENUS: A series of missions to Venus have revealed details of the planet and its atmosphere. One of the goals of the Soviet Venera space program was to achieve a soft landing on the planet. The first few *Venera* spacecraft were crushed by the pressure of the atmosphere. Then, in 1970, *Venera 7* successfully touched down on the planet. Other probes followed. They took photographs, examined soil samples, and conducted experiments on the planet's surface.

Landers are unable to provide a broader picture of the planet's surface. Both Soviet and U.S. space probes have flown above the planet and carried out radar-mapping programs. The American spacecraft *Magellan*, launched in May 1989, has provided the most recent information.

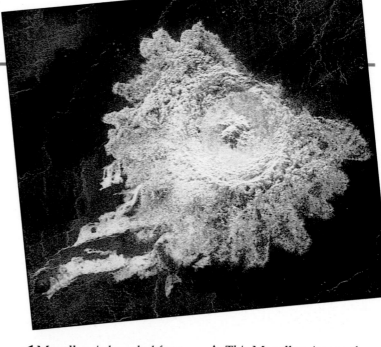

◄ Magellan *is launched from the space shuttle on its journey to Venus. The probe carried out an extensive radar-mapping mission of the planet.*

▲ *This* Magellan *image of Venus reveals a complex crater 20 miles wide. A central peak, terraced walls, and circular rim can be seen.*

PLAINS AND PLATEAUS: Flat, rolling plains of boulders and rock cover more than half the surface of Venus. Certain parts of the planet have huge stretches of highland plateaus as large as Earth continents. In one northern region, Maxwell Montes rises higher than Everest—the tallest mountain on Earth. In a highland near the equator are volcanoes that may erupt, sending heat and gas into the atmosphere.

▼ *Venus lies hidden beneath dense clouds of sulfuric acid. The clouds circle the planet every four days.*

Temperatures in the ► atmosphere of Venus are hottest near the planet's surface. This image shows their range from hot (red) to cold (blue).

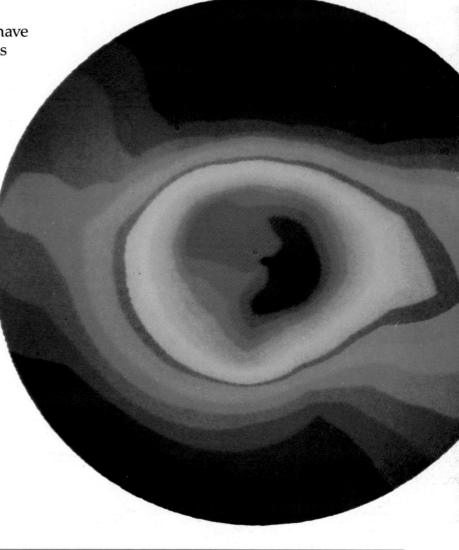

31

Mars

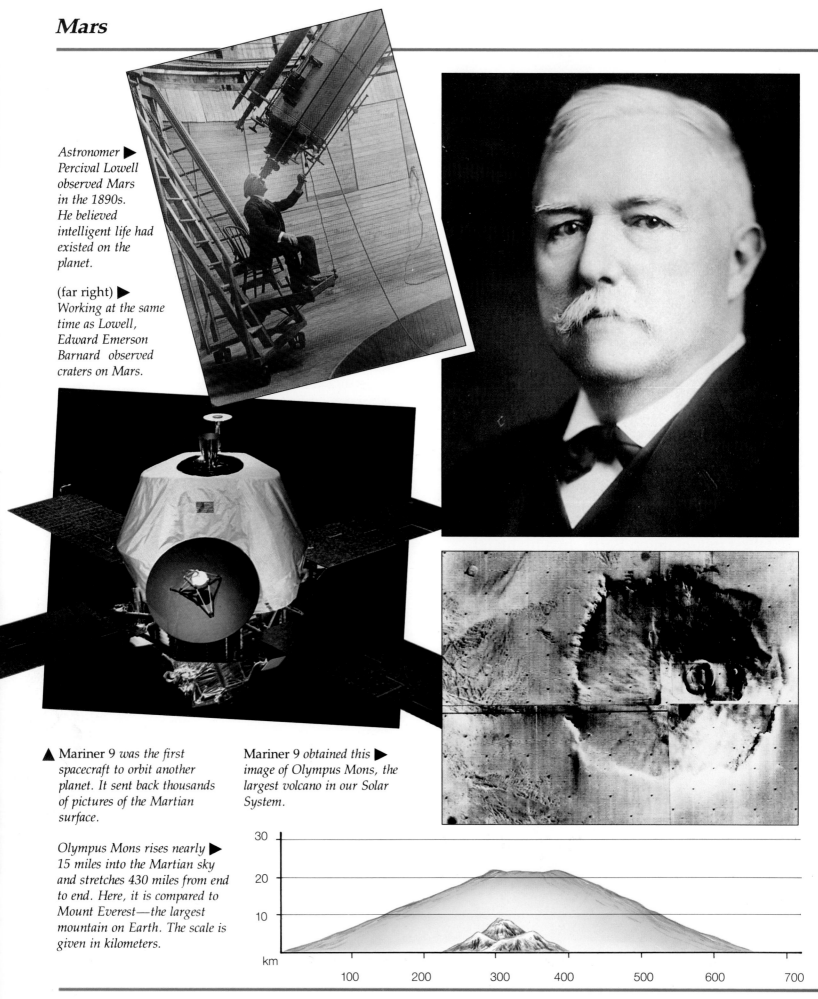

Astronomer ▶ Percival Lowell observed Mars in the 1890s. He believed intelligent life had existed on the planet.

(far right) ▶ Working at the same time as Lowell, Edward Emerson Barnard observed craters on Mars.

▲ Mariner 9 was the first spacecraft to orbit another planet. It sent back thousands of pictures of the Martian surface.

Mariner 9 obtained this ▶ image of Olympus Mons, the largest volcano in our Solar System.

Olympus Mons rises nearly ▶ 15 miles into the Martian sky and stretches 430 miles from end to end. Here, it is compared to Mount Everest—the largest mountain on Earth. The scale is given in kilometers.

No planet has captured people's imagination more than Mars has. At times, it appears in the Earth sky like a bright red star. Mars is not hidden by the Sun's glare like Mercury or shrouded in thick clouds like Venus. For more than a century, astronomers have pointed their telescopes at the Red Planet and wondered about what they saw.

SIGNS OF LIFE?: One popular idea was that life existed on Mars. American astronomer Percival Lowell studied the planet in the 1890s. He reported seeing over 150 straight lines crisscrossing the Martian surface. Lowell believed an intelligent civilization had dug these canals. In this desert world, he thought they used the canals to transport water that was frozen at the polar ice caps.

Other scientists disagreed with Lowell's theory. Modern astronomers with more powerful telescopes could not find any of the canals Lowell saw. They did notice that the surface changed color from season to season. Could this be caused by plant life on the planet?

In recent times, space probes sent to the planet disapproved these theories. They found no evidence of the canals or of plant life. So far, there is no proof to suggest life has ever existed on Mars.

SPACESHIPS TO MARS: In 1965, *Mariner 4* flew past the planet and sent back 21 pictures of its surface. Two *Mariner* probes followed, providing additional fleeting views of the surface. In November 1971, *Mariner 9* went into orbit around Mars. Over the next 11 months, the probe took more than 7,000 images of the Martian surface.

Although the *Mariner* probes found no canals on the Martian surface, they did reveal many interesting details. Mars is a dusty, cratered planet that resembles the Moon more than Earth.

There are several spectacular features on the Martian surface. A group of huge volcanic mountains rises from a part of the planet just north of its equator. Among them is Olympus Mons—the largest volcano in our Solar System. Equally spectacular is the Valles Marineris. This extensive network of canyons and valleys stretches for thousands of miles.

The *Mariner* probes greatly expanded our knowledge of Mars. They also laid the groundwork for the soft landing of spacecraft on the Martian surface.

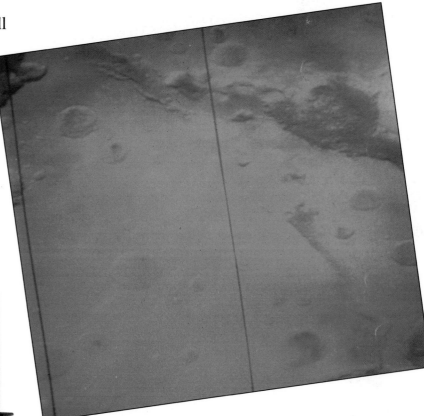

◄ *Soviet technicians work on one of two* Phobos *probes that were launched in 1988. The spacecraft were designed to study Mars and its two moons—Phobos and Deimos.*

▲ *The* Phobos *probes were unable to complete their planned missions. Before losing contact,* Phobos 2 *sent back this picture of the Martian surface.*

The Viking Missions to Mars

The next major step in the exploration of Mars was the landing of two spacecraft on its surface. The probes were part of the Viking space program. Scientists launched *Viking 1* in August 1975; *Viking 2* followed one month later. Both spacecraft reached Mars the following summer.

Each craft had two parts—an orbiter that would fly around the planet and a lander designed to touch down on its surface. Although the probes were expected to operate for about three months, they worked much longer. The orbiters transmitted over 55,000 images. Scientists used these pictures to map the planet.

THE LANDERS REACH THE SURFACE: The *Viking 1* lander touched down in Chryse Planitia, a lightly cratered, rocky lowland area. *Viking 2* set down almost on the opposite side of the planet at Utopia Planitia. In this flat region of fractured plains, few craters were found.

Scientists on Earth could communicate directly with the *Viking* landers. They guided them through a series of activities and experiments. The probes snapped color pictures of the surface. They measured wind speed and air temperature, and analyzed the Martian atmosphere. Using a long robotic arm, each lander scooped up samples of soil to be tested for signs of life.

Photographs received from the *Viking* landers showed that the sky has a reddish tint, a result of fine dust floating in the atmosphere. The Martian atmosphere has proved to be incredibly thin. It is made up mostly of carbon dioxide. There are tiny traces of other elements thought to be essential to life, including nitrogen, carbon, and oxygen.

THE SEARCH FOR LIFE: Each *Viking* lander carried out biological experiments to test the planet for signs of life. The soil picked up by robotic arms was injected with nutrients. If simple life-forms such as bacteria lived in the soil, they would absorb the "food" and give off gases as waste.

When the experiments were completed, *Vikings'* sensitive instruments had detected no release of gases. That does not mean life never existed on Mars or that it is entirely lifeless now. Still, the odds of finding life there in the future remain slim.

▲ *The* Viking 1 *spacecraft begins its journey to Mars aboard a Titan rocket in 1975. Ten months later, the* Viking 1 *lander touched down on the Martian surface.*

▼ Viking 1 *took this picture of Mars. Particles of rusty iron oxide in the planet's soil give Mars its red color.*

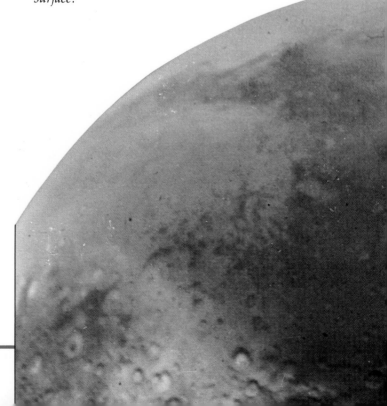

A Viking 1 *picture of the* ▶ *Martian surface. The rocks are typical of those found on lava fields on Earth.*

▼ Viking 1 *took this remarkable picture of a Martian sunset. Dust hanging in the atmosphere tints the sky red.*

▲ *A full-scale model of a* **Viking** *lander. The probes studied the land and weather conditions on Mars. Scientists on Earth communicated directly with the landers.*

◀ *A photograph of a part of the spectacular Valles Marineris. This huge rift, or canyon, runs along the Martian equator. If it were placed on the United States, it would stretch from coast to coast.*

The Viking 1 *sampler arm is* ▶ *seen against the rocky, red Martian landscape. Controlled by computer, the arm collected soil samples that were analyzed on board the lander.*

5 The Outer Planets

Beyond Mars and the Asteroid Belt lie the outer planets. They include the four huge, gaseous worlds of Jupiter, Saturn, Uranus, and Neptune, plus tiny Pluto. The four gas giants are also called the Jovian planets after Jupiter—the largest planet of all. (In Roman mythology, the god Jupiter was also known as Jove.)

The outer worlds of our Solar System are made up mostly of hydrogen and helium. The material that makes up these planets is much less dense than that of the inner, terrestrial planets. Saturn, for example, is so light that the entire planet would float in water!

SWIRLING CLOUD COVER: The colorful pictures we see of the Jovian planets show cloud patterns in the upper layers of their atmospheres. High winds create zones, or bands, of color that move around the planets. The bands are particularly colorful around Jupiter and Neptune.

The swirling gases of the upper atmospheres extend down tens of thousands of miles toward the planets' surfaces. Scientists believe the planets have solid cores. These centers contain materials such as iron, silicon, and magnesium. The cores may be similar in size to the entire Earth.

PROBES TO THE OUTER PLANETS: A series of successful space missions provided scientists with dramatic photographs and detailed data on the Jovian planets. In March 1972, *Pioneer 10* was launched. It reached Jupiter in December 1973 and flew within 40,000 miles of the planet. The probe studied Jupiter's atmosphere and observed at close range several of its moons. *Pioneer 11* flew within 13,000 miles of Jupiter and then continued on for a look at Saturn.

Following the success of the *Pioneer* probes, *Voyager 1* and *Voyager 2* were sent to the outer planets. *Voyager 1* flew past Jupiter and Saturn. *Voyager 2* swung past both planets and then provided the first detailed looks at Uranus and Neptune.

▲ *The* Voyager 1 *spacecraft heads for its encounter with Jupiter in March 1979. The probe sent back dramatic pictures of the planet and four of its moons.*

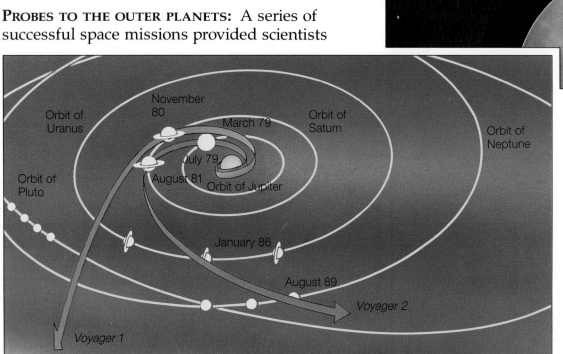

◄ *This diagram shows the flight paths of the* Voyager *spacecraft.* Voyager 1 *swept past Jupiter and Saturn.* Voyager 2 *reached all four gas giants. Eventually, the two spacecraft will fly out of our Solar System.*

▲ *The colorful Jovian cloud belts are beautifully displayed in this* Voyager 1 *image. Io, one of Jupiter's moons, passes in front as it orbits the planet.*

◀ *This* Voyager 2 *image of Saturn was taken from a range of 21 million miles in July 1981.*

▲ *This* Voyager 2 *image was taken during the approach to Neptune in August 1989. Bright clouds are seen over the Great Dark Spot.*

▲ Voyager 1 *reached Saturn in November 1980. The probe took pictures of the satellites (moons) Titan, Dione, Rhea, and Mimas.* Voyager 2 *followed in August 1981. It sent back information about Iapetus, Hyperion, Tethys, and Enceladus.*

THE OUTER PLANETS					
Planet	Diameter miles (km)	Distance From Sun miles (km)	Sidereal Period (year)	Axial Rotation Period	Number of Satellites
Jupiter	88,846 (142,980)	483,400,000 (778,000,000)	11.86 years	9.84 hours	16
Saturn	74,846 (120,540)	886,700,000 (1,427,000,000)	29.46 years	10.23 hours	18
Uranus	31,765 (51,120)	1,783,400,000 (2,870,000,000)	84.01 years	17.30 hours	15
Neptune	30,777 (49,530)	2,794,000,000 (4,497,000,000)	164.79 years	17.83 hours	8
Pluto	1,429 (2,300)	3,666,000,000 (5,900,000,000)	248.00 years	6.3874 days	1

Jupiter

Jupiter appears to us as a bright yellow star in the night sky. When viewed through an average-size telescope, it is about the same size as our planet's Moon. Four of Jupiter's moons are large enough to be seen from Earth with the aid of binoculars.

Jupiter is by far the largest planet in our Solar System. Its diameter is about one-tenth that of the Sun. Jupiter weighs over twice as much as all the other planets combined. It takes up so much space that more than 1,000 Earths could fit inside it easily!

THE GREAT RED SPOT: The upper region of Jupiter's atmosphere is made up of bands of colorful clouds that are continually changing. One fairly constant sight is the Great Red Spot. This swirling oval storm is often as wide as three Earths. It is so large that it can be viewed by telescope from our planet. The Great Red Spot was first seen in 1665 by Italian astronomer Gian Domenico Cassini.

AN OCEAN OF HYDROGEN: Jupiter's upper atmosphere is made up mostly of hydrogen gas. Thousands of miles closer to the planet's center, the layers of hydrogen are squeezed by the enormous pressure from above. Under this incredible pressure, the compressed gas turns into liquid hydrogen. An ocean of hydrogen covers the planet. Scientists believe there is a small core made up of rock and iron somewhere beneath all the liquid.

RINGS AND MOONS: Prior to the arrival of the *Voyager* probes, astronomers had identified twelve moons orbiting Jupiter. The spacecraft discovered an additional four moons. They also revealed an unexpected surprise—a system of rings circling the planet.

Jupiter's ring system is not nearly as spectacular as the one seen around Saturn. Its main section is about 4,000 miles wide and 20 miles thick. A faint inner band reaches down almost to the cloud tops in Jupiter's upper atmosphere. Outside the main section lies a fainter band. It reaches out to a distance of 62,000 miles from the planet.

GALILEO TO FOLLOW: *Voyager 2* flew within thousands of miles of Jupiter's atmosphere. Soon scientists hope for an even closer look at the planet. A new probe named *Galileo* has been designed to explore the planet's atmosphere. *Galileo* will release a probe that will descend by parachute into Jupiter's atmosphere. It will radio back detailed information about the planet, before being crushed and destroyed by Jupiter's intense pressure.

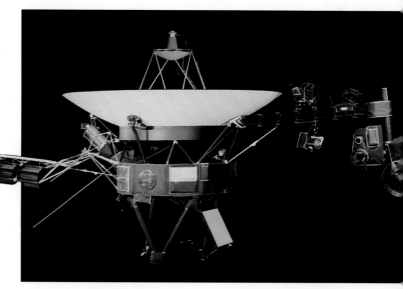

◀ Voyager 1 *lifts off on September 5, 1977. In March 1979, the probe flew within 300,000 miles of Jupiter.*

▲ *The* Galileo *spacecraft sits on board the space shuttle Atlantis. The Galileo project includes an orbiter and a probe, which will descend into Jupiter's atmosphere.*

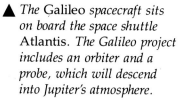

◀ Voyager 1 *discovered Jupiter's ring system during its March 1979 encounter.*

▲ *A* Voyager 1 *image of Jupiter shows its colorful bands of clouds. The Great Red Spot appears south of its equator.*

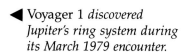

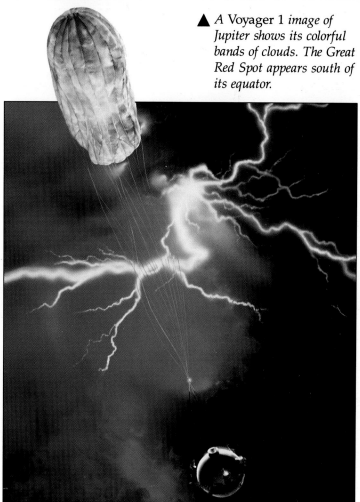

◀ *This view of the* Voyager *space probe shows the platform on the right where its cameras and scientific instruments are mounted.*

▲ *This close-up* Voyager *image focuses on Jupiter's Great Red Spot.*

This artist's impression ▶ *shows an atmospheric probe at work.*

The Moons of Jupiter

Jupiter has a total of sixteen satellites. Its four largest moons orbit the planet at its equator. Io, Europa, Ganymede, and Callisto are known as the Galilean satellites. They were discovered in 1610 by the Italian astronomer Galileo Galilei. The *Voyager* spacecraft studied these four moons closely and revealed each to be a unique world.

VOLCANIC IO: About the same size as Earth's Moon, the surface of Io is a brightly colored mixture of yellow, orange, white, and black. Io has two kinds of active volcanoes. Some shoot plumes of sulfur dust and gas over 100 miles into space. Lava flows out of others, covering regions of this moon and changing its features. Io is the only moon in our Solar System with active volcanoes.

FROZEN EUROPA: Europa, slightly smaller than Io, is the brightest of the Galilean satellites. This moon is covered by a layer of ice that is 60 miles thick. There are no mountains or craters on its smooth surface. Instead, its icy crust is broken up by a pattern of long, dark streaks that run for thousands of miles. They give the satellite its unusual cracked appearance.

GROOVED GANYMEDE: The largest moon in our Solar System is slightly larger than the planet Mercury. Craters cover much of Ganymede's icy crust. Other areas of the moon have large dark patches. Grooves and ridges appear in patterns across its surface, giving Ganymede a wrinkled look.

CRATERED CALLISTO: Only slightly smaller than Ganymede, Callisto is one of the most heavily cratered worlds in our Solar System. Its dark surface of ice and dust has almost no smooth regions. Callisto looks as it did billions of years ago.

THE SMALLER MOONS: The other satellites of Jupiter are divided into three groups. Metis, Adrastea, Amalthea, and Thebe orbit the planet inside the orbit of Io. As with the Galilean satellites, they travel around Jupiter more or less at its equator.

Jupiter's eight other moons are farther from the planet. Leda, Himalia, Lysithea, and Elara orbit 7 million miles from Jupiter. Ananke, Carme, Pasiphae, and Sinope are between 13 million and 15 million miles away. These moons may well have been tiny minor planets captured and held by Jupiter's gravity.

◀ *In this montage, Callisto (lower right), Ganymede (lower left), Europa (center), and Io orbit Jupiter.*

▼ *In this* Voyager 2 *image, a huge dark area dominates the lower right portion of Ganymede. It is called Galileo Regio.*

▲ A color-enhanced image shows an eruption of the volcano Loki on Io. The plume of sulfur reaches up almost 125 miles above the moon's surface. Loki is one of several active volcanoes discovered on Io.

▼ A view of Ganymede shows a banded region on its surface. Inside the bands are channels that probably were formed by movements in Ganymede's icy crust following a large meteoritic impact.

▼ Europa has an icy surface covered with huge cracks or fractures. These extend for several thousands of miles in every direction. Some of the cracks are 45 miles wide.

▼ This view of Callisto reveals its highly cratered surface. The craters suggest the surface crust has undergone little change since it formed some 4 billion years ago.

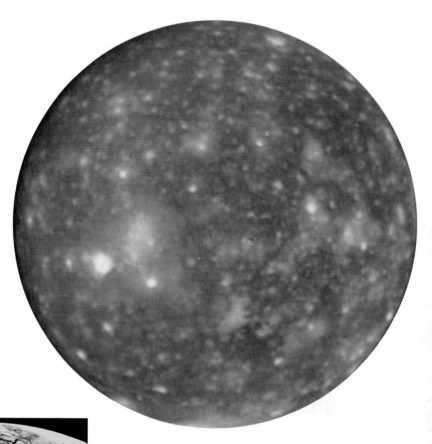

▼ The surface of Europa is smooth and contains very few craters. Several dark areas have been found to be more uneven.

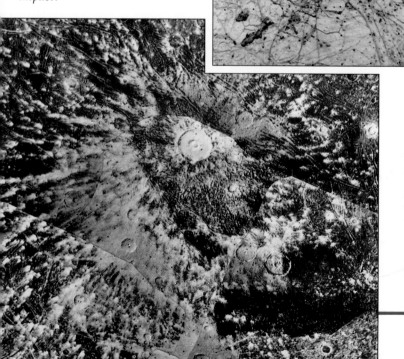

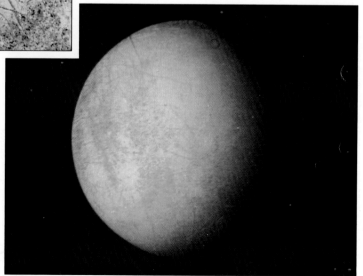

Saturn and Its Rings

Saturn, the second largest planet in our Solar System, is twice as far from Earth as Jupiter is. It often appears as a dim point of light in our night sky. When viewed through a high-powered telescope, however, its appearance is spectacular. A beautiful system of rings circles the planet.

Saturn's upper atmosphere contains bands of clouds moving around the planet. The clouds are a softer, creamier color than the ones around Jupiter. There are no giant storms to match Jupiter's Great Red Spot. Much smaller spots are seen at times. Like its larger neighbor, Saturn appears to possess a layer of liquid hydrogen and a rocky core.

A PLANET WITH EARS: Galileo was the first person to view Saturn's ring system. Through his telescope, the planet appeared to have cuplike ears on each side. Galileo was puzzled by this. He wondered if the planet had moons that hovered in one place rather than orbiting the planet.

Fifty years later, another astronomer named Christiaan Huygens viewed Saturn with a more powerful telescope. He could see that Saturn's "ears" were actually a system of rings continually circling the planet.

▼ This *Voyager 1* image was taken after the spacecraft left Saturn. The Sun's light shows day and night on the planet. Saturn's shadows darken a section of its rings.

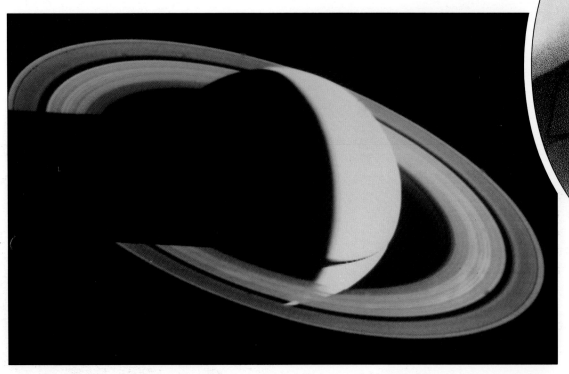

▲ The rings of Saturn contain several divisions. The area lying within the A ring is called the Encke Division. It was discovered by Johann Franz Encke in 1837.

◀ Faint belts and zones are clearly seen on Saturn. This Voyager 2 image was taken from 27 million miles away.

▼ A close-up view of the rings of Saturn taken by Voyager 2. The variation in color is caused by the different chemical makeup of each ring.

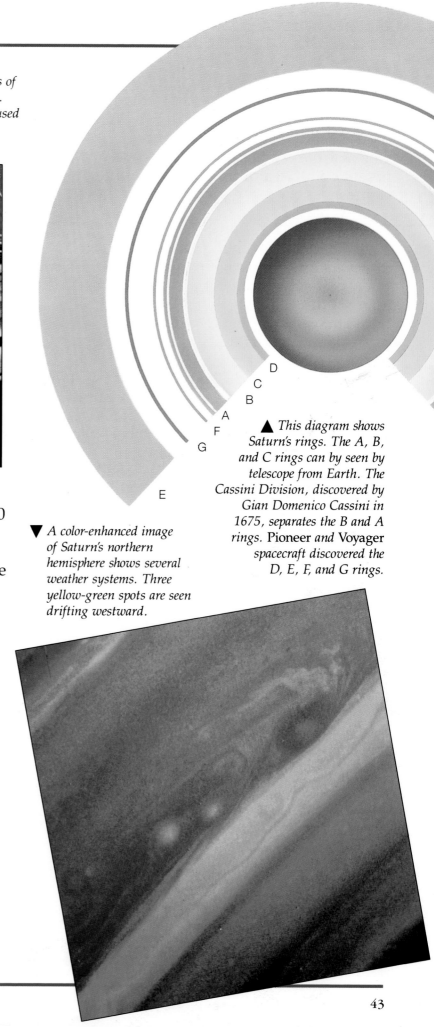

▲ This diagram shows Saturn's rings. The A, B, and C rings can by seen by telescope from Earth. The Cassini Division, discovered by Gian Domenico Cassini in 1675, separates the B and A rings. Pioneer and Voyager spacecraft discovered the D, E, F, and G rings.

▼ A color-enhanced image of Saturn's northern hemisphere shows several weather systems. Three yellow-green spots are seen drifting westward.

THIN, ICY RINGS: Saturn's rings begin about 30,000 miles above the planet and stretch 170,000 miles into space. They are made up of dust and particles of ice. Most particles are tiny, but there are also huge, wide boulders of ice. The rings are never more than a few hundred yards thick.

The rings are made up of several separate bands. From Earth, telescopes reveal three distinct regions: the brightest B ring, the less bright A ring, and the faint inner C ring. Two clear spaces have also been detected. The Cassini Division separates the A and B rings. The Encke Division is located within the outer regions of the A ring.

Spacecraft sent to Saturn have added to the number of known rings. *Pioneer 11* discovered the F ring, located just outside the A ring. *Voyager* cameras sighted the D, E, and G rings. The D ring is found between the planet and the C ring. The extremely faint E and G rings are located well outside the main ring system. The *Voyager* cameras also revealed many new details of the rings. For instance, the F ring appears to have braids and twists in it.

The Moons of Saturn

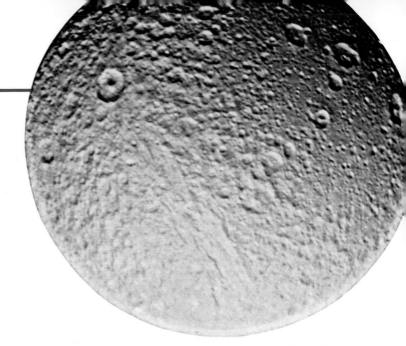

Before the arrival of spacecraft from Earth, ten satellites were known to orbit Saturn. Images sent back by *Pioneer 11* and the two *Voyager* craft revealed several more moons. Those discoveries, plus new observations using telescopes on Earth, have raised the number of satellites to at least eighteen.

HAZY TITAN: By far the best known and most intriguing moon is Titan. This satellite was discovered by Christiaan Huygens in 1655. Titan is a planet-size moon that is slightly larger than Mercury. It is the only moon known to have a thick atmosphere. Titan's hazy atmosphere is made up mostly of nitrogen, with smaller amounts of methane, argon, and other gases.

Titan's unseen surface remains a puzzle. It may be covered by a layer of methane. The surface is so cold that the methane may be in liquid or frozen form. In the future, astronomers hope to learn more about this mysterious moon. Scientists are designing a new spacecraft named *Cassini*, which will lower a probe onto Titan's surface.

SEVEN MEDIUM-SIZE SATELLITES: Saturn has seven more moons of moderate size. Each has a rocky core and an icy crust. Mimas, one of the smallest of the seven, orbits nearest Saturn. It has a huge crater named Herschel that is 81 miles across—one-third the diameter of that entire moon. Enceladus has a smooth surface with

grooves and fault lines. Many of its icy craters may melt because of this moon's heating up in some mysterious way.

Tethys is home to the largest crater on any of Saturn's moons. Named Odysseus, it is 250 miles wide and 10 miles deep. The other side of Tethys has a huge, 1,250-mile-long trench, named Ithaca Chasma. It may have formed from shock waves during the impact that created Odysseus.

Rhea is second in size to Titan and the most heavily cratered moon in Saturn's system. Dione features craters, faults, and valleys on its surface. Dione appears to share its orbit with another, smaller moon named Dione B.

The two most distant medium-size moons are Iapetus and Phoebe. Iapetus has one bright, icy side and a darker side. Little is known about Phoebe, which was far from view by *Voyager* cameras.

ODD SHAPES AND SHEPHERDS: Most of Saturn's other satellites are small, irregularly shaped objects. The largest are Janus and Hyperion. Three small satellites named Pandora, Prometheus, and Atlas are called shepherd moons. Their gravitational forces appear to help hold together the A and F rings.

◀ *Saturn is surrounded by six of its larger satellites. Saturn has more moons than any other planet in our Solar System.*

The Cassini *spacecraft mission may one day explore Saturn. It will orbit the planet. Cassini's probe will land on Titan's surface.* ▶

Tethys is a heavily cratered moon. Also visible on the satellite's surface is Ithaca Chasma, a huge canyon that is 1,250 miles long.

A Voyager image of ▶ Dione shows a surface peppered with craters. Dione's surface also displays many other features.

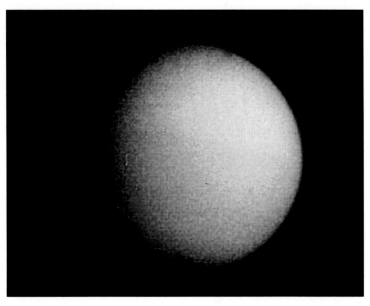

▲ *Cloud bands cover Titan. Saturn's largest satellite is the only moon in our Solar System with a thick atmosphere.*

Enceladus is the smoothest ▶ of Saturn's moons. Like Jupiter's moon Ganymede, it has grooves on its surface.

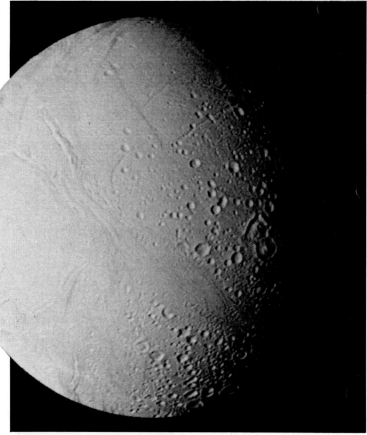

◀ *Rhea has the most craters of any of Saturn's satellites. Its largest craters probably formed shortly after Rhea itself. Its many smaller ones were made by the impacts of pieces of space debris.*

Uranus

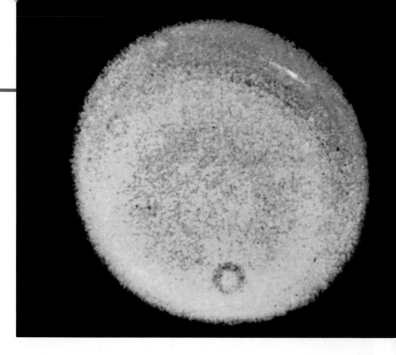

At one time or another, every planet from Mercury to Saturn is visible from Earth with the naked eye. For centuries, these six planets were thought to be the limit of our Solar System. Even after the refracting telescope was invented, over 170 years passed before a new planet was seen.

AN ACCIDENTAL DISCOVERY: Uranus was discovered quite by chance. On the night of March 13, 1781, astronomer William Herschel was observing stars in the constellation of Gemini. Herschel noticed that one "star" was not like the others. Through his telescope, this greenish object appeared to be shaped like a disk.

Herschel watched the disk move across the sky for several nights. At first, he thought he had discovered an unknown comet. Yet once the disk's orbit was determined, he realized he had stumbled across a new planet. Orbiting the Sun at twice the distance of Saturn, Herschel's discovery, Uranus, doubled the size of the known Solar System.

Like the other gas giants, we can only see the upper atmosphere of Uranus. This region is made up of hydrogen and helium with traces of other gases. Scientists believe the planet has a solid rocky core. Surrounding the core is a thick layer of atmosphere containing water, methane, and ammonia.

The oddest feature of Uranus is its tilt. The planet is turned on its side so that its north and south poles are in line with the Sun. The result of this peculiar position is a long period of uninterrupted daylight. During its 84-year-orbit around the Sun, there are 42 years of daylight followed by 42 years of darkness!

In January 1986, *Voyager 2* flew past Uranus. Its cameras revealed a banded atmosphere, similar to those of Jupiter and Saturn, although not as impressive. A number of methane clouds were seen floating over the southern part of the planet. The temperature at the top of these clouds was a chilly -346° F.

NEW RINGS AND MOONS: *Voyager 2* also provided a detailed view of the planet's system of rings, which had been seen from Earth in 1977. Those earlier observations had identified nine rings. The results from *Voyager 2* increased the number of major rings to eleven. The system of rings extends between 23,000 and 32,000 miles from Uranus. *Voyager 2* also discovered ten previously unknown satellites orbiting Uranus. The planet is now known to have at least fifteen moons.

William Herschel was an ▶ amateur astronomer when he discovered the planet Uranus in 1781. After that, astronomy dominated his life.

◄ Voyager 2 *recorded this image during its encounter with Uranus. The probe's pictures found no distinctive cloud patterns to match those seen on Jupiter or Saturn.*

▼ *This view spans the ring system of Uranus and shows all the main rings. Computer enhancement makes the rings appear much brighter than they really are.*

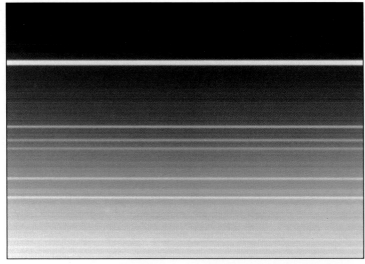

▲ *In this combination of two pictures, Uranus and its ring system appear above the surface of the satellite Miranda.*

▲ *This parting view of Uranus was taken by* Voyager 2 *as it passed the planet and headed on toward Neptune. Uranus appears as a thin crescent lit from behind by the distant Sun.*

An artist's impression shows ► Voyager 2 *heading for its encounter with Uranus. The probe flew for more than eight years before reaching the planet.*

The Moons of Uranus

Before the arrival of *Voyager 2*, five moons were known to orbit Uranus. The two largest, Titania and Oberon, were discovered by William Herschel in 1787. Five years later, Herschel identified one more satellite, which was named Umbriel. Ariel was sighted in 1851, and Miranda was located in 1948. The photographs sent by *Voyager 2* reveal these moons to have many similarities.

ICY, CRATERED MOONS: Oberon orbits at the farthest distance from Uranus. Its icy surface is covered with many craters. Some of Oberon's large, bright craters have dark centers. They may have been flooded by a dark, rocky material that flowed like lava from the moon's interior.

Titania, Uranus's largest satellite, appears grayish in color. It orbits the planet at a distance similar to the Moon's distance from Earth. Titania has an icy, cratered surface. Fault lines, valleys, and large cracks run across portions of the satellite.

Umbriel is the darkest of the moons. Its ancient surface is covered with overlapping craters. Its most interesting feature is a bright ring that is 90 miles wide. This ring may be the bottom of a large crater.

Ariel is similar in size to Umbriel. Several bright craters are seen on its surface. Valleys, faults, and broken lines crisscross the satellite. Glaciers of ice may have flowed from some of its valleys.

Miranda orbits nearest Uranus. The small satellite appears to be the most interesting moon of all. *Voyager 2* cameras revealed a large number of geological features, including mountains, cliffs, canyons, and plateaus. Miranda has craters and grooved patterns cut into its surface, too.

THE NEW MOONS: *Voyager 2* identified ten more moons orbiting Uranus. The first and largest new satellite discovered was Puck. It has a dark, cratered surface that is similar to those of the previously known satellites.

The instruments and cameras on *Voyager 2* tracked each of the new satellites for a period of time. Although their approximate size and orbits have been calculated, little else is known about them.

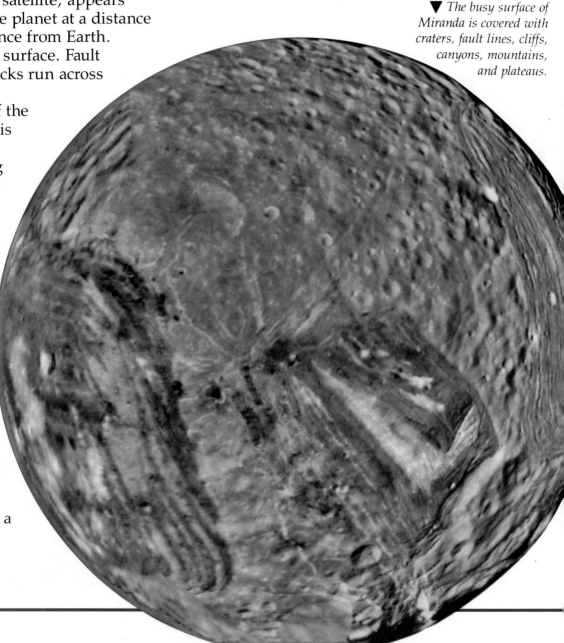

▼ *The busy surface of Miranda is covered with craters, fault lines, cliffs, canyons, mountains, and plateaus.*

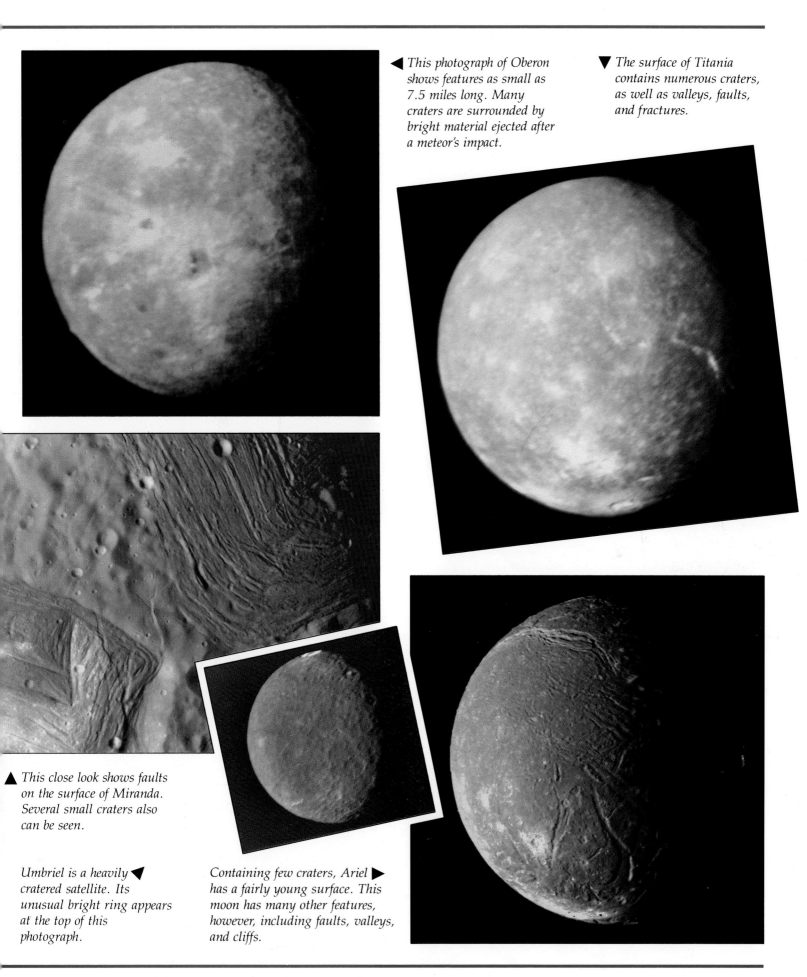

◀ This photograph of Oberon shows features as small as 7.5 miles long. Many craters are surrounded by bright material ejected after a meteor's impact.

▼ The surface of Titania contains numerous craters, as well as valleys, faults, and fractures.

▲ This close look shows faults on the surface of Miranda. Several small craters also can be seen.

Umbriel is a heavily ▼ cratered satellite. Its unusual bright ring appears at the top of this photograph.

Containing few craters, Ariel ▶ has a fairly young surface. This moon has many other features, however, including faults, valleys, and cliffs.

Neptune

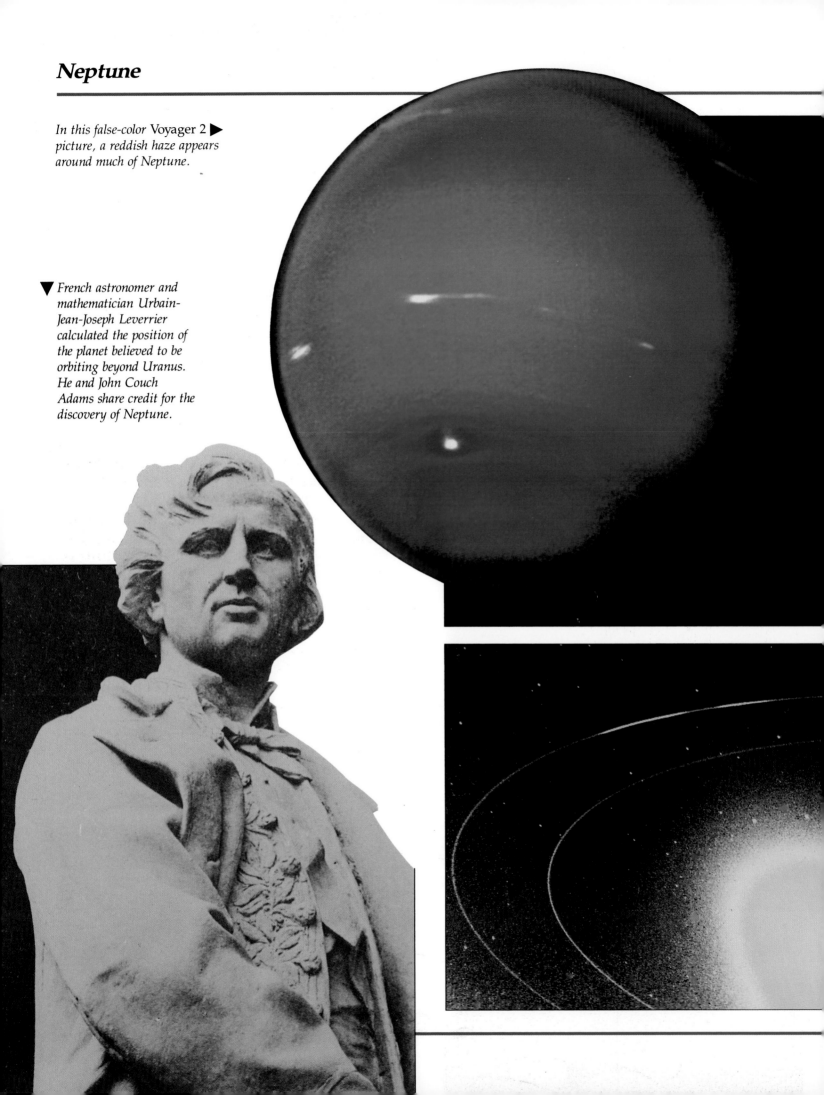

In this false-color Voyager 2 ▶ picture, a reddish haze appears around much of Neptune.

▼ French astronomer and mathematician Urbain-Jean-Joseph Leverrier calculated the position of the planet believed to be orbiting beyond Uranus. He and John Couch Adams share credit for the discovery of Neptune.

After the discovery of Uranus, 65 years passed before another planet was located in our Solar System. Then, in 1846, astronomers found Neptune.

SEARCHING FOR NEPTUNE: Astronomers suspected that an eighth planet existed before anyone actually found it. Scientists tracking Uranus in its orbit around the Sun watched the planet wander a bit off its predicted path. They thought the gravitational attraction of a more distant planet was tugging it off course.

In France, mathematician Urbain-Jean-Joseph Leverrier studied the orbit of Uranus. He calculated the location of the unseen eighth planet from the Sun. Using his figures, scientists found Neptune. Another mathematician, John Couch Adams, had performed similar calculations at the same time. Today, Leverrier and Adams share credit for the discovery of Neptune.

In August 1989, after having left Uranus three and a half years earlier, *Voyager 2* flew past Neptune. From this vast distance, the spacecraft sent information to Earth. Traveling at the speed of light, *Voyager's* radio signals took more than four hours to reach our planet!

◄ *Above Neptune, two bright rings appear lit by the Sun's light. The planet's faint third ring cannot be seen in this picture.*

▼ *Wispy cirrus clouds of frozen methane drift above Neptune. Its main cloud deck lies 30 miles below.*

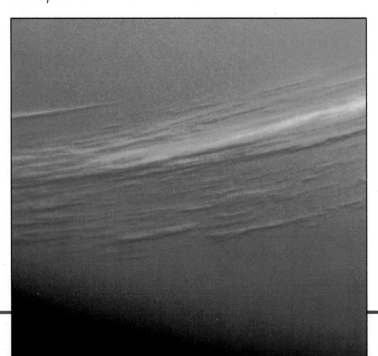

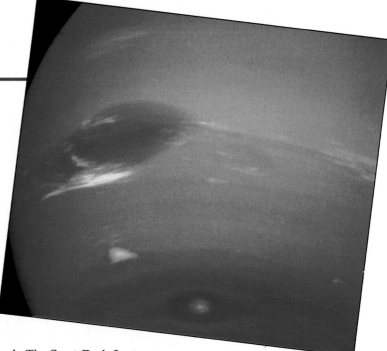

▲ *The Great Dark Spot appears in Neptune's atmosphere. A bright patch of frozen methane and the Small Dark Spot also can be seen.*

ANOTHER GAS GIANT: Neptune is similar in size to Uranus. Like the other Jovian planets, it is made up mostly of hydrogen and helium. *Voyager 2* cameras revealed an active Neptunian atmosphere with bands and zones crossing the disk. Beneath its upper atmosphere, Neptune is thought to consist of a layer of melted ice surrounding a rocky core.

Many cloud features were also seen. Most notable was the Great Dark Spot. This huge, oval storm cloud is about the size of Earth. A second storm—the Small Dark Spot—was also seen. These regions seem to be holes in the cloud cover, which reveal lower regions of the planet's atmosphere.

Wispy streaks of clouds appear above Neptune's main cloud system. These cirrus-type clouds were seen in many areas, including over the dark spots. They appear to be made up of frozen methane.

For some time, it was widely believed that Neptune had a system of rings. Cameras on board *Voyager 2* confirmed this. The planet's ring system is made of three narrow bands. The two brightest rings lie 23,600 miles and 17,000 miles above Neptune's cloud tops. A third, much fainter, ring was found 10,500 miles from the planet.

The Moons of Neptune

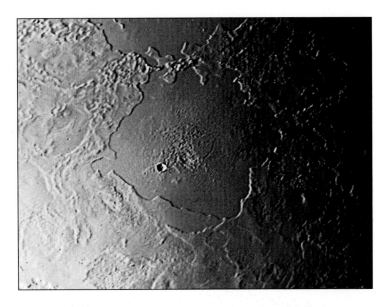

▲ *This heavily cratered moon discovered by Voyager 2 cameras is called satellite 1989N1. It is slightly larger than Nereid.*

▲ *Smooth areas similar to those on our Moon are seen on Triton. These probably formed following volcanic eruptions, when lava flowed out to form flat, smooth "seas."*

An artist's impression shows ▶ *Voyager 2 approaching Neptune for its final encounter. Seen to the lower left is the planet's largest satellite. Triton.*

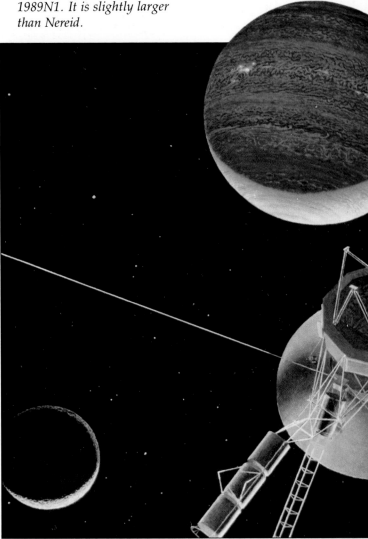

◀ *This image of Triton reveals a number of surface features, including cracks and craters. Its pink color stretches from the southern polar region.*

This image was taken as ▶ *Voyager 2 approached Neptune. The spacecraft was still 47 million miles from its target. Triton appears in the lower right corner.*

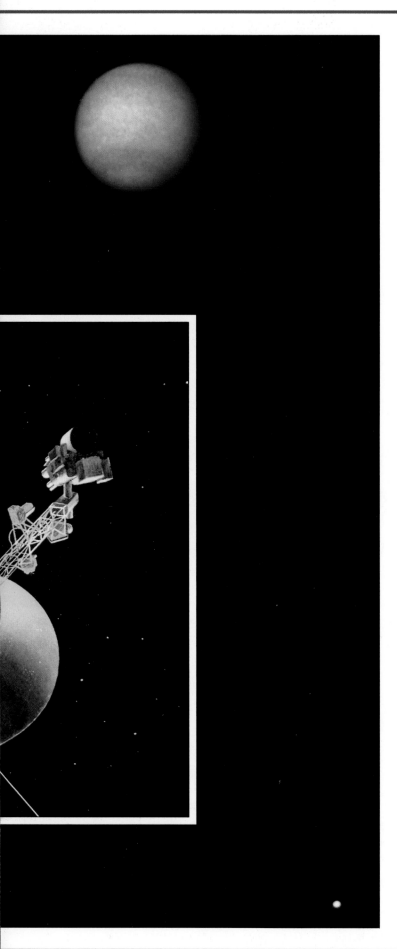

Triton is Neptune's largest satellite. It was discovered by astronomer William Lassell in 1846, less than three weeks after the discovery of Neptune itself. A second small moon, called Nereid, was found 100 years later by Gerard Kuiper. *Voyager 2* located six more moons during its encounter with Neptune.

A BACKWARD ORBIT: Triton is one of the biggest moons in our Solar System. It is slightly larger than the planet Pluto. Triton may well have been an independent body captured by the gravity of Neptune. Triton is about 220,000 miles from that planet's surface. It has a peculiar backward orbit as it circles the planet from east to west.

Voyager 2 images revealed Triton as a fascinating world. Its surface displays a wide assortment of geological features. Fault lines and craters cover much of its icy surface. Smoother areas, caused by flowing lava, also can be seen.

A bright polar ice cap stretches nearly halfway to Triton's equator. When atomic particles from the Sun strike the methane ice there, it turns pinkish. Some ice from the surface also may melt and escape into Triton's atmosphere. A thin layer of methane and nitrogen gas has been detected around the planet.

One of the most dazzling features *Voyager 2* spotted were ice volcanoes. These geysers appear to shoot liquid nitrogen from underground pools. The nitrogen rises 25 miles into the atmosphere, freezes, and is deposited on Triton's surface. The frozen nitrogen appears as dark streaks in *Voyager 2*'s photographs.

MYSTERIOUS NEREID: In spite of the *Voyager 2* visit, knowledge of the moon Nereid remains scanty. The tiny satellite has an unusually wide orbit. At its closest point, the *Voyager 2* craft was nearly 3 million miles from Nereid. The probe's cameras showed only a dark, featureless disk.

The six additional satellites discovered by *Voyager 2* range in size from about 30 to 250 miles in diameter. The largest of the new moons was actually found to be bigger than Nereid.

Pluto and Charon

The American astronomer Percival Lowell firmly believed in the existence of a planet beyond Neptune. For several years, he searched for it unsuccessfully. His efforts paved the way for the discovery of Pluto by Clyde Tombaugh in 1930.

This artist's imaginary view looks across the surface of Pluto. Its only satellite, Charon, is seen in the sky. Because of Charon's locked orbit, the moon always will appear at the same point above the planet's horizon.

Joining the gas giants far from the Sun is Pluto. The smallest planet in our Solar System is also the outermost one. It orbits the Sun once every 248 years.

Pluto's odd, oval orbit crossed inside the path of Neptune in 1979. Until 1999, Neptune will be the farthest planet from the Sun. No other planets cross orbits in this fashion. For this reason, some scientists think Pluto was once a moon of Neptune that broke away into its own planetary orbit.

THE SEARCH FOR THE NINTH PLANET: The story of Pluto's discovery is much like that of Neptune. After Neptune was discovered, scientists noticed that it, too, wandered slightly from its predicted path. Many felt the gravitational pull of a more distant planet might be the cause. One of the

▲ *The top picture, taken from a telescope on Earth, shows Charon as a bump on the side of Pluto. The lower image, taken by the Hubble Space Telescope, clearly shows planet and moon.*

▼ *Clyde Tombaugh peers into a device called a blink microscope comparator. He used it to compare star images taken a few days apart. This work led to his discovery of Pluto.*

astronomers who set out to try and find this as yet undiscovered planet was Percival Lowell. He searched unsuccessfully from 1905 to 1907.

Lowell's work paved the way for other astronomers, including Clyde Tombaugh. In 1929, a new wide-field camera was developed for taking pictures of stars in space. In 1930, after studying hundreds of photographs, Tombaugh found what he was seeking. One tiny, starlike point of light appeared in different positions on two photographs taken a few days apart. This "star" was behaving like a planet. A delighted Tombaugh announced that the ninth planet finally had been discovered.

Pluto is so far away and so small that information about the planet is very limited. Pluto is slightly smaller than the Neptunian satellite Triton. Like that moon, it is thought to be made up of rock and frozen gases. Methane frost has been detected on Pluto, which shows how cold it is. It is the only planet cold enough to have methane in frozen form. Pluto has a thin atmosphere that also is made up of methane.

PLUTO'S ONLY MOON: In June 1978, the American astronomer James W. Christy discovered a satellite orbiting Pluto. Christy noticed a bump on Pluto's image. Similar bumps had been noticed on several earlier photographs. In some cases, these appeared on the opposite side of Pluto. Christy realized that the bump was a satellite. It was so close to Pluto that it could only be seen at the farthest point in its orbit from the planet. The satellite was named Charon.

Charon is about a third the size of Pluto. More than any other pair in our Solar System, this planet and moon are locked together. The same side of Charon faces Pluto at all times. On average, the satellite orbits at a mere 11,350 miles from the planet. For these reasons, Pluto and Charon are sometimes thought of as a double planet.

6

The nine planets and their moons are only a few of the bodies in our Solar System. Scientists have detected thousands of other objects moving in orbit around the Sun. Many of them are asteroids. These are also known as minor planets, or planetoids.

The largest asteroids measure a few hundred miles in diameter. Several of these are round like planets. The more common, smaller asteroids look like tumbling chunks of rock. The greatest number of asteroids orbit the Sun between Mars and Jupiter. This region is known as the Asteroid Belt.

THE SEARCH FOR THE "MISSING PLANET":

In 1766, a mathematician named Johann Titius made a prediction about where new planets might be found. According to his calculations, a planet should exist somewhere in the large space between Mars and Jupiter. His work was revived and published six years later by astronomer Johann Bode.

At first, astronomers were skeptical of the Titius-Bode Law. However, when Uranus was discovered beyond the orbit of Saturn, its location also fit the formula. Astronomers began to search for the "missing planet." The first discovery was made by the Italian astronomer Giuseppe Piazzi in 1801.

Piazzi noticed a faint object in the constellation of Taurus. Unlike a star, it moved slightly from night to night. Piazzi concluded that the object was in orbit. Since it was the correct distance from the Sun, Piazzi thought he had found the missing planet. Piazzi named the object Ceres.

Over the next few years, three more objects—Pallas, Juno, and Vesta—were found at about the same distance from the Sun. As more bodies were discovered, it became clear that there was no missing planet between Mars and Jupiter. There were thousands of objects.

The minor planets of the Asteroid Belt may be part of a planet that failed to form during the early history of our Solar System. Jupiter's powerful gravity may have prevented another planet from developing near it.

A number of asteroids orbit out of the main region of the Asteroid Belt. The Trojans are two clusters of asteroids. They move in almost the same orbital path as Jupiter does. One group moves ahead of the planet and the other behind it.

ASTEROIDS AND EARTH:

About 80 asteroids that have been discovered come close to our planet. Amor asteroids approach Earth's orbit, while Apollo asteroids cross it. Another 80 asteroids, called the Atens, orbit between the Sun and Earth.

Occasionally Apollo asteroids come close to our planet. Among the so-called Earth grazers is Hermes. In 1937, this asteroid came to within 560,000 miles of Earth. Closer still came a tiny object called 1991BA. It came to within 106,000 miles of Earth in January 1991. That's over 100,000 miles closer than our Moon is to us!

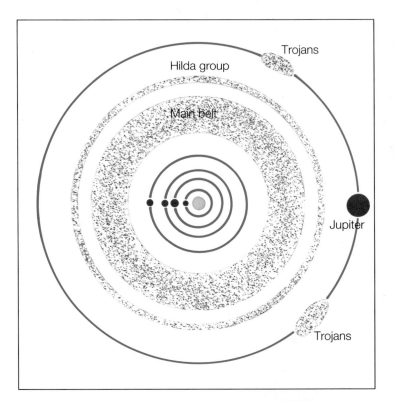

▲ *Most asteroids travel around the Sun between the orbits of Mars and Jupiter, within the main Asteroid Belt. There are many other groups, including the Trojans and the Hilda group shown here.*

THE FIRST 20 MINOR PLANETS

Number	Name	Year of Discovery	Discoverer	Diameter miles (km)	Orbital Period (year)
1	Ceres	1801	Piazzi	568 (914)	4.61
2	Pallas	1802	Olbers	324 (522)	4.61
3	Juno	1804	Harding	152 (244)	4.36
4	Vesta	1807	Olbers	311 (500)	3.63
5	Astraea	1845	Hencke	73 (117)	4.14
6	Hebe	1847	Hencke	119 (192)	3.78
7	Iris	1847	Hind	127 (204)	3.68
8	Flora	1847	Hind	94 (151)	3.27
9	Metis	1848	Graham	94 (151)	3.68
10	Hygiea	1849	De Gasparis	267 (430)	5.59
11	Parthenope	1850	De Gasparis	93 (150)	3.84
12	Victoria	1850	Hind	78 (126)	3.57
13	Egeria	1850	De Gasparis	133 (214)	4.14
14	Irene	1851	Hind	98 (158)	4.16
15	Eunomia	1851	De Gasparis	169 (272)	4.30
16	Psyche	1851	De Gasparis	164 (264)	5.00
17	Thetis	1852	Luther	67 (109)	3.88
18	Melpomene	1852	Hind	93 (150)	3.48
19	Fortuna	1852	Hind	133 (215)	3.82
20	Massalia	1852	De Gasparis	81 (131)	3.74

In order for a minor planet to be given a number, its discovery must be confirmed and an orbit worked out. Around 4,000 minor planets have now been catalogued with up to 200 further discoveries being added per year. Details for the first 20 minor planets to be discovered are given here, including each one's number and name, year of discovery and discoverer, diameter, and orbital period in years. These 20 minor planets orbit the Sun at a mean distance ranging from 204 million miles to 292 million miles (329-470 million km).

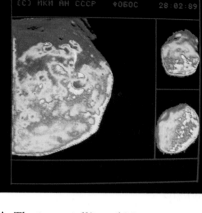

▲ The two satellites of Mars, Phobos and Deimos, may be asteroids that were captured by Martian gravity and pulled into orbit.

THE TITIUS-BODE LAW

In 1766 the German mathematician Johann Titius brought to light an interesting numerical relationship linking the distances of the planets from the Sun. Taking the numbers 0, 3, 6, 12, 24, 48 and 96 (each of which, apart from 3, has a value twice that of the previous number), he added 4 to each. This gave values of 4, 7, 10, 16, 28, 52 and 100. Nothing remarkable here, you might say! However, if you then divide these figures by 10, the result gives the approximate distance of each planet from the Sun in Astronomical Units (1 Astronomical Unit is the average distance between the Earth and the Sun).

Planet	Distance given by law	Actual distance (AU)
Mercury	0.4	0.39
Venus	0.7	0.72
Earth	1.0	1.0
Mars	1.6	1.52
—	2.8	—
Jupiter	5.2	5.2
Saturn	10.0	9.54

Titius noticed that there was no planet tying in with the value 2.8 and he suggested that an as-yet-undiscovered planet was orbiting the Sun between Mars and Jupiter. Astronomers doubted this, even when the German astronomer Johann Bode publicized the idea again in 1772. However, opinions changed in 1781 after the discovery of Uranus. Carrying the sequence on, Uranus would lie at a distance of 19.6 according to the Titius-Bode Law, very close to the actual value of 19.18!

A diagram taken from a ▶ French scientific magazine published in 1891 shows the relative sizes of the largest asteroids. Note that in the drawing, Vesta is larger than Ceres. This is incorrect. Ceres, the first asteroid to be discovered, is also the largest found to date.

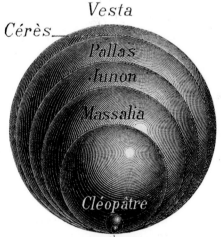

Vesta
Cérès
Pallas
Junon
Massalia
Cléopâtre
Agathe

◀ This medallion honors three astronomers who discovered many asteroids. They are John Russell Hind, Hermann Goldschmidt, and Robert Luther.

The Comet Rendezvous and ▶ Asteroid Flyby (CRAF) mission is being planned for a launch in the 1990s. One of the probe's targets will be the asteroid called Hamburga.

Comets

▲ Halley's comet has been seen for centuries. Here it is shown in the Bayeux tapestry. When it appeared in 1066, it was considered a bad omen.

Edmond Halley predicted ▶ that the bright comet he observed in 1682 would return in 1758. When it did, the comet was named in his honor.

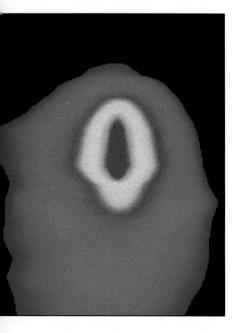

▲ This image shows the comet named IRAS-Araki-Alcock. In 1983, it was discovered by the Infra-Red Astronomy Satellite (IRAS). The blue color in this image shows material escaping to form the comet's tail.

Astronomers at the Catalina ▶ Observatory obtained this photograph of a comet named Kohoutek in January 1974.

The appearance of a comet near Earth is often a spectacular event. A great comet may stretch across the night sky. A comet may be the brightest object in the sky. It may glow brilliantly for weeks or months before disappearing in space.

Comets are actually small members of our Solar System. At the center of a comet is a head, or nucleus, that measures several miles across. A comet's head is made up of ice, rock, and dust. Because of this mixture, comets sometimes are described as "dirty snowballs." Comets' tails are made up of gas and dust. A single comet often has two or more tails.

HOW COMETS FORM: The Sun and its planets occupy a relatively small part of our Solar System. A vast cloud of material is thought to lie beyond the orbit of Pluto. This cosmic debris includes icy chunks left over from the time when our Solar System formed. The cloud is called Oort's Cloud. It is named after astronomer Jan Oort, who first suggested that it existed.

The comets we see probably start in Oort's Cloud. Gravity from a passing star may cause a chunk of icy rock to break free. The force may propel the comet toward the inner regions of our Solar System. When a comet approaches the Sun, the heat from our star acts upon it. The ice within the comet vaporizes. It releases dust and gas, which form a glowing cloud around the nucleus, called a coma.

As the comet approaches, the effect of the Sun increases. Solar winds blow material away from the head of the comet. A long stream of gas or dust stretches to form the tail. Often a comet has one dust tail and one gas tail.

Comets' tails can be thousands, or even millions, of miles long. Because they are blown by solar winds, tails always point away from the Sun.

After rounding the Sun, comets swing back toward the outer reaches of our Solar System. Farther from the Sun's heat and energy, the coma and tail disappear. They will re-form when the comet passes near the Sun again. With each solar trip, a comet loses some of its material. Over time, it appears less bright than when it first was seen.

▲ This picture shows the nucleus of Halley's comet. The photograph was built up from a series of images. They were taken by the Giotto spacecraft.

▼ Halley's comet has been a regular visitor to our skies for thousands of years. This photograph was taken during its return in 1910.

LONG-DISTANCE TRAVELERS: Comets travel in deep orbits around the Sun. Most take many years to complete a single orbit. About 400 comets have been discovered that orbit the Sun within 200 years. These are considered short-orbit comets. Others are in such deep orbits that they may take thousands of years to complete a single trip.

By far the most famous short-orbit comet was named for Edmond Halley. Its arrival has been recorded in artwork and records that are centuries old. Halley's comet appears every 75 to 76 years. Its most recent arrival was in 1986.

Probes to Halley's Comet

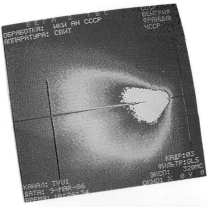

◀ *This color-enhanced image shows Halley's comet. It was taken by the* Vega 2 *probe, the second of two Soviet probes to pass near the comet.*

▼ *A* Vega *spacecraft is seen here before launch. The* Vega *missions explored both Venus and Halley's comet.*

Although comets have been observed for many centuries, our knowledge of them has been limited. The arrival of Halley's comet early in 1986 presented a unique opportunity. It was the first time since the beginning of the space age that Halley's comet passed near Earth. Scientists around the world spent years preparing for its arrival. As Halley's comet approached our planet, five separate probes were sent to meet it.

VEGA ARRIVES FIRST: The Soviet Union sent two spacecraft to Halley's comet. *Vega 1* and *Vega 2* first flew to Venus. After lowering experiments into that planet's atmosphere, they flew to intersect the comet. The *Vega* craft reached Halley's comet on March 6 and March 9, 1986. From a distance of about 5,000 miles, they sent back pictures and other data to scientists on Earth.

Japan also launched two probes. These were the first spacecraft ever sent by that country into deep space. *Sakigake* came within 4.3 million miles of the comet on March 11, 1986. Its main aim was to investigate the interaction between the solar winds and the comet. The *Suisei* probe came even closer. It passed within 94,000 miles of the

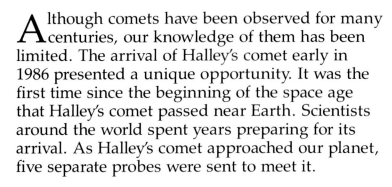

comet on March 8, 1986. It examined the shell of hydrogen gas that surrounded the head of the comet.

GIOTTO **IS CLOSEST:** By far the most successful probe was *Giotto*, which was launched by the European Space Agency. Using images sent back by the *Vega* craft, scientists targeted *Giotto* for the closest encounter of all. The probe flew to within 380 miles of the nucleus on March 14, 1986.

As *Giotto* approached the glowing coma and nucleus, there were tense moments on Earth. A tiny dust particle hit the spacecraft, knocking its antenna out of alignment. Contact between Earth and *Giotto* was lost for about 30 minutes. When communication was restored, the probe successfully completed its work.

The nucleus of Halley's comet was seen in a series of photographs. It appeared as a very

In August 1985, ▶ Suisei *became the second Japanese probe sent to intercept Halley's comet.*

dark, irregularly shaped chunk of ice. It was nine miles long by five miles wide. Several features were seen on the surface of the nucleus. One of these was a series of vents. Gas and dust seemed to leave the nucleus from these vents. This material formed the comet's coma and its tail.

FUTURE ENCOUNTERS: Halley's comet will not return until about the year 2061. In the meantime, scientists are planning to look closely at other comets. One effort involves reusing *Giotto*. The probe has been redirected by scientists on Earth. It is scheduled for another encounter with a comet named Grigg-Skjellerup in the near future.

In the United States, a future mission is being planned by NASA. Its name is the Comet Rendezvous and Asteroid Flyby, or CRAF. Plans may include flying with a comet's nucleus for a long period of time. A lander may even set down on a comet's nucleus.

◄ Vega 2 *was launched in December 1984. It reached Venus in June 1985 and Halley's comet nine months later.*

▲ *The* Giotto *probe was built by the European Space Agency. It made the most successful encounter to date with Halley's comet.*

Meteors and Meteorites

Meteors equal to, or ▶ brighter than, Venus are known as fireballs. The path of a fireball lights up this nighttime exposure. To its left is the Andromeda Spiral galaxy.

▼ *The Leonid meteor shower is particularly active every 33 years. In this engraving, the 1833 Leonid shower fills the sky in spectacular fashion.*

A bright, bursting meteor ▶ appears at the bottom of this photograph. Above it is the constellation Orion.

▼ *This Arizona meteorite crater has a diameter of nearly a mile. It was formed thousands of years ago following the impact of a meteorite 650 feet in diameter.*

◀ *This meteorite weighs 745 pounds. It is one of the largest meteorites ever recovered from an observed fall.*

At times, starlike points of light may suddenly streak across the night sky. These bright streams of light often are called shooting stars. Although they look like stars, they are really tiny particles called meteors.

SPEEDING BITS OF DUST: Floating in space are bits of dust and rock called meteoroids. As Earth orbits the Sun, some of this debris wanders too close to our planet. When the force of gravity draws these bits into our atmosphere, they are known as meteors.

Meteors travel incredibly fast—up to 44 miles per second! They collide with air molecules. Friction is produced and the meteors burn up before reaching the ground. That burning light is what we see as a shooting star.

SHOWERS IN THE SKY: Meteors may appear at any time. On certain nights, however, the sky seems filled with them. These meteor "showers" are caused by the dust of comets. As a comet orbits the Sun, it loses material, which it leaves in its path of orbit. Earth passes through the paths of certain comets at particular times of the year. With so much dust in Earth's path, the number of meteors seen from our planet increases. During some showers, as many as 50 meteors can be seen every hour.

Rarer than meteor showers are spectacular meteor storms. On these nights, thousands of meteors appear in the sky every hour. Meteor storms are particularly active showers. Many are associated with the dust in the path of a comet called Tempel-Tuttle. The next storm in this path is scheduled to reach our planet on November 17, 1999.

REACHING EARTH: Meteorites are rocky fragments that broke off of asteroids. These larger objects enter Earth's atmosphere and reach our planet. Some meteors leave large impact craters when they strike Earth.

Meteorites are much less common than meteors. Only a small number are detected in a given year. The largest meteorite on display in a museum is the 31-ton object at the Hayden Planetarium in New York. The largest known

meteorite weighs around 60 tons. It lies where it fell at Hoba West, in South West Africa.

Like Moon rocks, meteorites are about 4.5 billion years old. They are the remains of the material that formed the planets during the development of our Solar System.

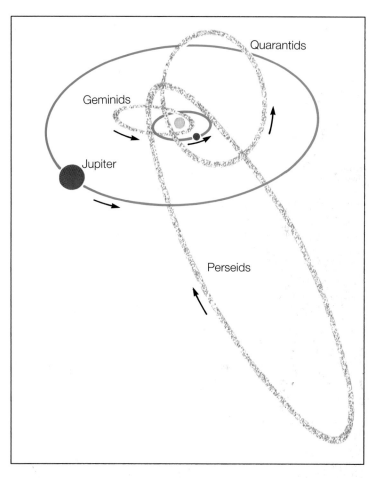

▼ *At times, Earth feels the impact of a large object. In 1908, a piece of comet nucleus hit Earth's atmosphere above Siberia.*

▲ *Meteor showers are caused by streams of meteoroids orbiting the Sun. Three well-known streams are shown here. The orbits of Earth and Jupiter are also pictured.*

Further Reading about Our Solar System

Furniss, Tim. *Journey Through Space.* New York: Gallery Books, 1991.

Jones, Brian. *Exploring the Planets.* New York: Gallery Books, 1991.

Lauber, Patricia. *Journey to the Planets.* New York: Crown Publishers, 1986.

Moore, Patrick. *Exploring Earth and Moon.* New York: Gallery Books, 1991.

Ridpath, Ian. *Astronomy.* New York: Gallery Books, 1991.

Whitfield, Philip. *Why Do Volcanoes Erupt?* New York: Viking Penguin, 1990.

Picture Credits

The publishers would like to thank the picture agencies and photographers who supplied the photographs reproduced in this book. With the exception of the photographs detailed below, all photographs were supplied by the Public Information Offices of **NASA** and the **Jet Propulsion Laboratory, Pasadena, California.** Pictures are credited by page numbers.

American Museum of Natural History, Department of Library Services: 8 bottom left, 9 bottom right, 32 upper left; 62 top right, 63 lower. **The Bettmann Archive:** 7 top, 12 upper left and lower right, 62 middle left. **Boeing Aerospace:** 29 upper left. **Peter Bull Art Studio:** 4–5 (artwork), 5 (artwork), 6 (artwork), 11 (artwork), 12 (artwork), 13 (artwork), 16 (artwork), 26 (artwork), 32 (artwork), 36 (artwork), 43 (artwork), 56 (artwork), 63 (artwork). **EOSAT:** 23 lower right. **Hansen Planetarium, Salt Lake City, Utah:** 10. **Hughes Aircraft Company:** 30 lower. **Lowell Observatory, Flagstaff, Arizona:** 59 lower. **Ann Ronan Picture Library:** 28 upper and lower right, 56 lower, 57 middle. **Starland Picture Library:** 4 (artwork by Julian Baum), 10–11 (Colin Taylor/FAS), 12 lower left (Richard Barnett/FAS), 19 lower left (NASA), 22 upper (Hughes), 22 lower (ESA), 23 upper right and lower left (EOSAT), 24 lower (ESA), 25 lower left (ESA), 27 upper right (NASA), 28 lower left (Yerkes Observatory), 29 lower right (NASA), 31 upper right (NASA/JPL), 32 upper right (Yerkes Observatory), 46 lower (Yerkes Observatory), 50 lower (Yerkes Observatory), 54–55 (artwork by Julian Baum), 55 upper (ESA), 55 lower (Lowell Observatory), 59 upper (ESA), 62 lower left (Yerkes Observatory), 62 middle right (Andrew Sefton/FAS). **Tass/Sovfoto:** 15 upper left, 17 upper left, 30 upper, 33, 57 upper, 60 upper, middle, and lower. **Yerkes Observatory, University of Chicago:** 54.

Cover pictures: NASA (front, all images); Peter Bull Art Studio (back).

Index